"Nancy Guthrie speaks to the person in need of courage. She urges us to look down less and up more. Grabbing on to his hope is our only hope—this book prompts us to do just that."

MAX LUCADO
Pastor and *New York Times* bestselling author

"Nancy knows the comfort and sufficiency of God's goodness and love in the midst of loss and grief. Many have benefited from her transparent and biblical response to her sovereign journey. Many have heard her strong testimony of trust and confidence in her foundation of faith—Christ Jesus the Lord. Hoping for Something Better *will lift our gaze to look at Jesus, quickening our praise, adoration, and worship of Him who alone is worthy. Study and embrace the strong meat of this portion of God's Word as found in the book of Hebrews as it 'fits you' for the course laid out for your journey of faith."*

JANE PATETE
Women's Ministries Coordinator, Presbyterian Church in America

REFUSING TO SETTLE FOR LIFE AS USUAL

hoping for something better

Nancy Guthrie

TYNDALE MOMENTUM™

The nonfiction imprint of Tyndale House Publishers, Inc.

Visit Tyndale online at www.tyndale.com.

Visit Tyndale Momentum online at www.tyndalemomentum.com.

Visit Nancy Guthrie's website at www.nancyguthrie.com.

Tyndale, Tyndale's quill logo, *Tyndale Momentum*, and the Tyndale Momentum logo are registered trademarks of Tyndale House Ministries. Tyndale Momentum is a nonfiction imprint of Tyndale House Publishers, Carol Stream, Illinois.

Hoping for Something Better: Refusing to Settle for Life as Usual

Designed by Jessie McGrath

Published in association with the literary agency of Alive Communications, Inc., 7680 Goddard Street, Suite 200, Colorado Springs, CO 80920.

For information about special discounts for bulk purchases, please contact Tyndale House Publishers at csresponse@tyndale.com, or call 1-800-323-9400.

Library of Congress Cataloging-in-Publication Data

Guthrie, Nancy.
Hoping for something better : refusing to settle for life as usual / Nancy Guthrie.
p. cm.
Includes bibliographical references.
ISBN 978-1-4143-1307-8 (sc)
1. Bible. N.T. Hebrews—Devotional literature. 2. Christian women—Prayers and devotions. I. Title.
BS2775.54.G87 2007
248.8′43—dc22 2007004460

Printed in the United States of America

27 26 25 24 23 22
14 13 12 11 10 9

Dedication

I lovingly dedicate this book to the women of Christ Presbyterian Church in Nashville, Tennessee. How vividly I remember the first time I went away with you for a retreat in 1994. I'd never been around so many women who wanted to know God so intimately and walk with him so closely. I saw in you a passion and commitment I didn't have, and you made me want it. Your lives showed me there was something better.

I thank you for sharing the unexpected joys and deep sorrows of life with me over these years together. Thank you for giving me the space and time to be sad and the freedom to be me with all my flaws. And I thank you most of all for allowing me the privilege of standing before you to teach the book of Hebrews. You can't imagine how thrilling it was for me—the culmination of a long-term dream and the birthplace of this book.

Contents

God had planned something better for us. . . .

HEBREWS 11:40

foreword

Is it really all about Jesus?

Back in the mid '60s when I first embraced him, I would tell people it was all about Jesus, but I had no idea what that meant. Sure, Christianity was centered on Christ, but mainly he was the one who got my spiritual engine started. As long as I filled up on Jesus every morning during my quiet time, I was able to putter along just fine, thank you.

Things changed in the late '60s after I crushed my spinal cord in a diving accident that left me a quadriplegic. I felt desperate and afraid. *Oh God, I can't do this. I can't live like this!* My engine would sputter and die before the day even started. I felt small and fragile. Vulnerable. Hopeless. This time I needed him urgently. Every hour. Every minute. *Or else I'll suffocate, God!* I was beginning to see that life really is all about Jesus.

Somewhere in the '70s I realized that the Bible is all about him too. I would read how "Jesus is in the Old concealed; in the New, revealed." So I spent hours sitting in front of God's Word—especially the Old Testament—flipping this way and that with my mouth stick, hoping to catch a glimpse of him in Genesis or Jeremiah, Leviticus, or Lamentations. If I could but find Jesus in the whispers and omens between those ancient pages, I somehow knew I'd gain a clearer, brighter picture of him. But it wasn't easy. Proverbs 25:2 was right: "It is the glory of God to conceal a matter."

The New Testament wasn't any easier. Flipping through the Gospels and Epistles, I finally landed upon the book of Hebrews. In the very first chapter I knew I had stumbled upon something pretty unique. Hebrews is the Bible commenting on itself, like a built-in, Spirit-inspired owner's manual, like a heaven-sent dictionary or commentary explaining just where and why the Savior is spoken of here, there, and everywhere throughout the timeless pages of the Word of God.

Hebrews provides the hieroglyphics of heaven. It speaks of a better country . . . a grand cloud of witnesses . . . a heavenly Jerusalem . . . and "thousands upon thousands of angels in joyful assembly." I liked that kind of talk. It was hopeful. In its pages, I was even able to crack the code behind the whispers and omens of why God had allowed my affliction. In Hebrews I found a home for my aching heart.

Now fast-forward some forty years, to the autumn of 2006. One night after I was situated in bed, my husband, Ken, pulled up a chair, reached for his glasses, and opened his Bible. We had been reading through the Bible as part of our nighttime routine, and that night he announced we had arrived at the book of Hebrews. I turned my head on the pillow and smiled—for the next few evenings I knew we'd be basking in the light of this most unusual and marvelous book. The next morning when I wheeled into my office, my smile grew brighter. There on my desk sat the manuscript for *Hoping for Something Better.* Wow. It was another homecoming for my heart.

Nancy Guthrie has composed a most excellent book, a wonderful guide into Hebrews. My friend possesses a unique authority to write the following pages for she, too, has suffered affliction. . . . She has cried, "Oh God, I can't live with this pain." . . . She has longed for hope and found it tucked between the paragraphs and chapters of Hebrews.

And friend, Nancy wants to help you crack the heavenly hieroglyphics. So get ready for an adventure. Watch what happens when you flick the switch on the spotlight of Hebrews and observe the way it illumines the dark and mysterious portions of the Holy Writ. Cup your ear and learn the language of all those God-breathed whispers from Deuteronomy and Daniel. Open your heart with each turn of the page, and feel it fill with hope.

I've lived in a wheelchair for four decades, and to tell you the truth, I'm looking for a better country: a place where death, disability, and disappointment are things of the past. It's natural to hope for something better. Sure, a better body and even a better heart. But most of all, that better country, that world—a new heaven and earth—that will atone for all our hurts and suffice for our tears. It will be a happy world where finally—oh glad and glorious day!—every tongue will confess that Jesus Christ is Lord.

Yes, it really is all about Jesus.

Joni Eareckson Tada
Joni and Friends International Disability Center
Winter 2007

were you hoping for something better?

I THINK SOMEONE SHOULD just be honest with brides and grooms, and it might as well be me. We're waiting for cake. We loved witnessing your vows and we enjoyed getting to hug you in the reception line and we endured the awkwardness of greeting all your relatives we've never met before, but now . . . we want cake.

Why is it that the bride and groom seem to take so long to cut the cake? What are they waiting for? Don't they know we came for cake!

I know there are some people reading this book who don't get this. You're in no rush at all. You have no yearning to savor the doughy goodness between layers of Crisco-sweet frosting because you've filled up on carrot sticks and little heads of broccoli. And amazingly enough to me, you're content with that and a few peanuts and cashews. But most of us are patiently awaiting the cutting of the cake, and we're hoping we can be near the front of the line without appearing overly anxious.

I think I accomplished this appearance of nonchalance at a wedding I attended recently. And as I went back to the table with my slice, everyone was talking about how delicious the cake was. But I have to admit, after all the waiting for that cake, it just wasn't what I was hoping it would be. It was a little light and spongy for me; the icing was more like whipped cream than real frosting; and it was filled with fruit. And I had to wonder if everyone else was just being nice—doing and saying what they've been trained by convention to do and say when they all smiled and said, "Isn't this cake delicious?"

The truth is, I had been waiting for and hoping for something better, something more satisfying to my sweet tooth. And I couldn't help but feel a bit disappointed.

DISAPPOINTMENT: A FAMILIAR FEELING

A sense of disappointment is a familiar feeling for most of us. There have been so many things that haven't lived up to their promise, someone else's sales job, or our own inflated, if not idealistic, expectations. We extend ourselves for the new house only to find that we can't enjoy it because of all the little things that are not quite right. We long for years to get married or to become parents only to find that family life is not always as idyllic as we imagined it would be. With each career goal we accomplish, we find out that there is always a downside to the dream and another hurdle to overcome.

> We are hoping for something authentic—something worth opening our hearts to and filling our minds with and giving our lives for.

In fact, because we've been so often disappointed, we've trained ourselves not to hope for so much, not to expect too much anymore. We'd rather not build ourselves up for what we see as an inevitable letdown. So we've learned to live expecting very little from other people, from ourselves, from life, even from God.

It's this disappointment with God, or with our experience or understanding of God, that creates real inner conflict. It seems so terribly unspiritual to admit that the Christian life, as we've experienced it so far, does not seem to really be what Jesus meant by "abundant life." It often feels as if we've missed it somehow, as if everybody else must be experiencing something we can't seem to achieve, but we don't want to admit it to ourselves or anyone else.

We find ourselves living with a nagging hope for something better. We want something better than the "churchianity" of our parents and grandparents; something better than the vague and uncertain spirituality of our neighbors; something better than guilt-induced, holier-than-thou morality; something better than here-and-now, health-and-wealth promises; something more than going-through-the-motions religiosity or the latest-fad religious experience. We are hoping for something authentic—something worth opening our hearts to and filling our minds with and giving our lives for.

We don't have to spend our whole lives on an endless and unsatisfying search. There really is something better that is within our grasp. Better than living life with a merely sentimental, superficial spirituality. Better than going through life with a debilitating fear of death. Better than becoming bored and burdened by meaningless religious ritual; better than feeling like an unwelcome outsider or an unworthy hypocrite; better than being bound by shame and regret. There is something better that makes problems worth persevering through, something that makes heaven worth waiting for, something worth running toward and dreaming of.

That something better is actually some*one* better: Jesus.

But even as I say it, whether or not you are a follower of Jesus, I know there is a voice inside you saying, *Oh, Jesus again,* or, *Just Jesus? Been there, done that.*

Because some of us have felt disappointed by Jesus, too—at least Jesus as we have understood him and experienced him to this point. Could it be that our desire for something better springs from our underestimation or devaluing of Jesus? Could it be that we've become so comfortable with the Jesus we've constructed that we just aren't that awed by him anymore and we've become blinded to what he is truly worth?

Could it be possible to move from wherever we are now to becoming more solidly convinced that Jesus is worth our costly devotion, our intellectual energy, our emotional investment, our cherished reputation, our everything? Could upping our amazement and affection for Jesus actually be the something better we've been looking for?

UNCOMFORTABLE WITH JESUS

Have you noticed that Jesus seems to make people nervous? When Jesus comes up in the conversation, things get weird. Somehow, while it may be fine to believe in God or be spiritual or even go to church, to talk about Jesus as real and relevant somehow crosses the line of acceptability in most circles.

Why is that? Why does Jesus make people so uncomfortable?

They needed encouragement to hang on to what is true–encouragement to place all their hopes for the future in who Jesus is and what he did.

Perhaps it's because while Jesus may be welcome at the table, he is welcome only as one religious option no greater than any other. The reality is, we live in a time of growing marginalization for those who identify themselves too closely with Jesus. They are just a little bit too radical, bordering on weird.

This was the kind of world the people who received the letter to the Hebrews in our New Testament were living in. Their conviction that Jesus was the Son of God—the sole way to knowing God in a saving way—put them at odds with the culture around them. Their relationship with Jesus and commitment to Jesus were being put to the kind of test all of us secretly hope we will never have to take and wonder if we would pass—the test of persecution. As a result of expressing belief in Jesus, they had been ostracized from the center of Jewish life—the Temple. They were estranged from their families, their businesses were blacklisted, and their homes and possessions were fair game. It was beginning to cost to follow Jesus—a cost that some of the Hebrew Christians were wavering on their willingness to pay.

They needed encouragement to hang on to what is true—encouragement not to settle for a socially acceptable kind of religion, encouragement to see Jesus in his superiority and sufficiency and to place all their hopes for the future in who Jesus is and what he did. It was seeing Jesus this way that would fill them with the courage and confidence they needed to stand strong. It is the same encouragement we need today.

When Jesus is small in our estimation, so are our courage and commitment. So seeing Jesus in all his beauty and significance will help us stand strong too, when life in this world is cruel and life in the next world seems distant and unreal.

A LOVING LETTER TO DISCOURAGED DISCIPLES

We don't know for sure who wrote this letter to the Hebrew believers and almost believers. We know he was an educated person, a seasoned preacher who knew the Old Testament. He knew the people he was writing to, and they knew him. And while it was sent in letter form, the book of Hebrews is really more of a sermon than a letter. The author addressed the Hebrews as listeners rather than readers.

This letter was likely sent to a house church in or around Rome, and when it arrived, the recipients likely gathered together and had someone read it out loud. So it was like a sermon in absentia given to second-generation believers and almost believers. Their parents had witnessed the signs, wonders, and various miracles of Jesus, but they hadn't—they'd just heard about them. They didn't have the firsthand memories of seeing Jesus in the flesh to gird them and give them courage when the going got tough.

And they began to wonder if following Jesus was really worth it. They wondered if they really needed to give up so much of what had defined them for so long. Judaism was based on God's revelation in the Old Testament, and it followed practices that were laid down and built upon through the centuries. And while these people believed in Jesus and wanted Jesus, they still had questions about following him and doubts about what they were leaving behind.

What about the Temple sacrifices and the priests? What about Moses and the prophets? Should they turn their backs completely on their religious heritage? Couldn't they cling to Christ and hold on to the ancient Jewish traditions too?

They missed the traditions. They missed the company and approval of their unbelieving family members who walked past them traveling to the Temple and to festivals. The old ways of seeking to earn God's acceptance by keeping the law and following rituals wooed them. These habits were comfortable and familiar and acceptable. The tug of tradition threatened to put these early believers in danger of developing a ceremonial, legalistic version of Christianity. Their desire to blend their belief in Christ with familiar Temple rituals revealed a lack of full confidence in the gospel, a lack of full confidence that Jesus himself is the fulfillment of all the ceremonies and sacrifices.

It wasn't just saying good-bye to the familiar that made following Christ difficult for these early believers. Christianity had not proven to be of worldly advantage to them. In fact, it set them up for persecution—for the loss of property, privilege, and perhaps even their lives. And they were not just being paranoid. Right around the time this letter was written, martyrdom became a reality of the Christian experience in Rome as Nero made Christians scapegoats to remove suspicion from himself after a great fire destroyed much of the city.*

These early Christians had lost their jobs and found themselves hungry—and worse, their children were hungry. They were objects of ridicule: Some people thought of Christians as cannibals because of what Jesus had said about eating his flesh and drinking his blood (see John 6:51-52). They were people like us, and naturally they were scared. So out of fear, some of them stopped associating with other Christians. Difficulty and loneliness and disappointment were slowly obscuring the truth of the gospel and tempting some toward compromise—or worse, complete renunciation of Christ.

As a result of their desire to cling to their religious rituals and their real fear of persecution, these believers were wavering. The distinctiveness of Jesus was getting fuzzy. They were wondering if they should play it safe and go back to Judaism with a little Jesus thrown in, or if they should keep moving forward with Christ, fully aware of the price they might have to pay for following him.

But then someone showed up with a letter, a letter from someone they knew and respected—a letter that was really more like a sermon. This letter reminded them why they had come to faith in the first place, reminded them of what made Jesus worthy of their worship and their very lives, reminded them of what was ahead for those who love Jesus and put all their hopes in him. This letter challenged and called them to keep on believing—to keep on persevering in the face of persecution and difficulty.

The book of Hebrews is an appeal for endurance in spite of difficulty, perseverance in the face of disappointment.

The book of Hebrews is an appeal for endurance in spite of difficulty, perseverance in the face of disappointment. In studying Hebrews, we find that considering Jesus—looking at him, valuing him, running after him, drawing near to him—is the secret to surviving and even thriving when life is hard. As we study the book of Hebrews together (through the pages of this book and in your personal or small group study using the Bible study for Hebrews at the

*According to R. Kent Hughes in *Hebrews: An Anchor for the Soul* (Wheaton, IL: Crossway, 1993), 1:19, the description of the persecution these believers had already experienced matches the hardships that came to Jewish Christians under Claudius in AD 49. At that time, Christians were expelled from Rome and banished from synagogues by the Jewish establishment. The author of Hebrews was likely writing around AD 64 or 65, when a new persecution was looming under Nero.

end of this book), we'll adopt three of the same goals the writer of Hebrews had when he sent this sermon-letter.

GOAL #1: TO GO DEEPER

Some of us have never really given that much thought to Jesus. We've never really invested energy and attention to examining who he is, what he said, and what he did.

Others of us are so familiar with Jesus that we take who he is and what he has done for granted. We've settled into a comfortable understanding of who he is, perhaps seeing him as less than he is.

We need to go deeper in our examination of who Jesus is and what he has done. Only then can we see that he is worthy of our devotion.

Jesus is amazing; he's stunning. And, as the writer to the Hebrews wants us to see, Jesus is better than anything or anyone or any way of getting to know God. He's the something better we've been hoping for. Throughout the book of Hebrews, we are told of the multitude of ways Jesus is better:

- He is better than the angels (1:4).
- He is better than Moses (3:3).
- He offers a better way of living out authentic faith (6:9).
- He holds out a better hope (7:19).
- He is the author of a better covenant (7:22).
- He is a better mediator (8:6).
- He makes better promises (8:6).
- He is a better sacrifice (9:23).
- He offers better and lasting possessions (10:34).
- He offers a better country—a heavenly one (11:16).
- He promises a better reward (11:26).
- He provides a better resurrection (11:35).

Better, better, better. Do you really believe Jesus is better? Is time with Jesus better than thirty minutes more sleep? More restful than a week at the beach? More interesting than your favorite magazine? Do you believe Jesus is smarter than your most intelligent relative or neighbor? More compelling than the latest philosophical fad? More reliable than a big insurance policy?

Would anyone looking at your life be able to see that you believe Jesus is better than anyone else and anything else this world has to offer?

Would they be able to tell that you love him? admire him? believe him? trust him? What evidence is there that you know him, that you are devoted to him?

Is it time for you to let go of every lesser savior so that you can embrace and enjoy someone better—Jesus? I'm not describing one brand of Christianity. This is where a real relationship, a saving relationship, with God begins.

Have you truly grabbed hold of Jesus? Perhaps you've never seen yourself before as someone who needs a Savior. You've never seen a need in your life for Jesus. Maybe you have seen church and religion and tradition but you haven't seen the real Jesus. Because when you see him for who he is, you will realize he is so good you can't resist him.

Will you allow this study of Hebrews to enlarge your understanding of, admiration for, and devotion to Jesus?

GOAL #2: TO DRAW CLOSER

What's the point of the Christian life, anyway? To guarantee a free ride to heaven? The work of Jesus on the cross was not just so that we could gain entry into heaven when we die. The Cross broke down the barrier between us and God so that we can draw near to him right now, today. So we can grow closer to him and go nearer to him. This is something better than staying on the fringes of relationship with God. It is the intimacy and authenticity you have been longing for.

> This is something better than staying on the fringes of relationship with God. It is the intimacy and authenticity you have been longing for.

The great theological teachings in Hebrews are not just to increase our theological knowledge; they are intended to serve as the basis for action. And the action the writer of Hebrews wants for his readers is to keep moving forward with God, toward God. He uses a combination of encouragement, instruction, and warning to prod us forward.

It is the same set of motivational tools parents use to get their kids to do what the parents know is best for their kids—a combination of encouragement, instruction, and warning.

Encouragement says, "Let's dive into that homework and get it done before dinner!"

Instruction says, "You must start your homework before dinner so you will have plenty of time to get it finished."

Warning says, "If you don't get your homework done before dinner, you will not get to watch your favorite TV program tonight."

The tone may be different, but the goal is the same—to get the homework done. And likewise, while the tone may be different throughout Hebrews, the goal is the same—to prod us to draw near to God through Jesus.

Throughout Hebrews, the writer encourages and instructs us with statements that begin with "Let us . . ."

Encouragement

- be diligent to enter God's rest (4:11)
- cling to him and never stop trusting him (4:14)
- draw near to the throne of grace with confidence (4:16)
- press on to maturity (6:1)
- draw near to God (10:22)
- hold fast the confession of our hope (10:23)

Instruction

- stimulate one another to love and good deeds (10:24)
- lay aside sin and legalism (12:1)
- run the race of faith (12:1)
- show gratitude to God (12:28)
- identify with the rejected Jesus (13:13)
- continually offer a sacrifice of praise (13:15)

Using phrases such as "do not" or "see to it that," he warns us against anything that will keep us from drawing near to God:

Warning

- pay more attention so you don't drift away (2:1)
- don't neglect your salvation (2:3)

- don't harden your heart (3:8)
- see to it that no one has an unbelieving heart (3:12)
- see to it that no one misses the grace of God (12:15)
- see that no one is sexually immoral or godless (12:16)
- don't refuse to listen to God speaking through Jesus (12:25)

The writer of Hebrews knows that because God extends his grace to us so freely, we can be lulled into a state of spiritual laziness, becoming comfortable with where we are and who we are. So he uses encouragement, instruction, and warning to stir in us a desire for something better, to keep us actively moving forward toward God. Hebrews challenges our superficial interpretations of the gospel that allow us to go easy on ourselves and each other. It shows us that the life of faith is rigorous and requires effort and attention—not so we can earn our salvation but so that we can enjoy the fullness of it here and now. The closer we get to God, the more we find we want of him, and we want to shed everything that is keeping us at a distance from him. And that shedding requires some effort on our part.

We can decide that because drawing near to God is what we want most of all, it will be worth examining ourselves, responding to the encouragements, following the instructions, and heeding the warnings we find in Hebrews.

The encouragements and instructions and warnings we will discover in more depth in our study of Hebrews were not only for the Hebrews; they are for us, too. We can decide that we will not take them all that seriously—that we will pick and choose the ones that appeal to us (perhaps as we think about someone else who needs to heed them). Or we can decide that because drawing near to God is what we want most of all, it will be worth examining ourselves, responding to the encouragements, following the instructions, and heeding the warnings we find in Hebrews.

For those of us who are followers of Christ, Hebrews will challenge us to set aside our old comfortable ways of approaching the Christian life, which require very little of us, so we can take up a new way of drawing near to God. It will require more discipline and more focus, but it will give us more rest and more joy.

If you have not yet chosen to follow Christ, Hebrews will challenge you to stop seeing Christianity as a club to join or a philosophy to follow and help you see that Christianity is about a person to draw near to—a person to hold on to throughout the ups and downs of this life, who will carry you safely into the next.

GOAL #3: TO HOLD TIGHTER

The writer of Hebrews knew he was talking to people who were already suffering, and he knew that their suffering for the cause of Christ was only going to increase in the days ahead. So he gave them the same encouragement that we need when difficulty sweeps into our lives: "Hold on. Don't give up. Keep a firm grasp on Jesus, no matter what comes."

These aren't empty words of motivation. They are based on something in the future that is sure and solid. The hope the writer of Hebrews talks about is the hope that Jesus has made a way for us to draw near to God in this life and that he will usher us into his very presence in the next. He is encouraging these early believers to hold on to the solid truth of the gospel that God saves sinners and has made a way for sinners to come to him. He's encouraging them to look forward to all that awaits them in eternity, and he wants that confidence to inspire endurance in the difficulties of living life on this earth.

How do we live as if Jesus is our only hope in this life and the next? Hebrews tells us:

- keep up our courage (3:6)
- keep on loving others (6:10-11)
- hold on to the security of God's promises (6:18)
- draw near to God (7:19)
- don't waver in unbelief (10:23)

Perhaps you have felt such a weight of disappointment that you have become disillusioned and discouraged. Perhaps you have toyed with the possibility of throwing in the towel on this whole faith thing. If so, the writer to the Hebrews invites you to hold tight, stand firm, and keep going. Don't we all need that kind of encouragement from the sidelines when life gets hard?

As I wrote about my wedding cake disappointment, I realized for the first time that there must have been some disappointed people at my wedding. We didn't even serve cake. Honestly I can't remember what I was thinking, except that we had a morning wedding followed by a brunch at a restaurant where they offered a variety of desserts. When we were planning our wedding, we thought people would enjoy having a variety of desserts to choose from rather than just cake. The restaurant surprised us with a little one to cut and feed to each other, but nobody else got any of it. And as I remember, it was pretty good. I wonder how many left our reception not quite satisfied and thinking, "I was hoping for something better. . . ."

And I wonder: Are you hungry enough for something better than what you've experienced so far that you will not only read the pages ahead but also complete the study of Hebrews at the end of this book? Oh, I hope so! That is a holy hunger—a hunger that God himself will satisfy.

There really is something better than wasting our lives and attention on the distractions this world offers. There is something better to be found in opening up the Word of God and expecting God to truly speak to us.

In the pages to come, as we work our way through the book of Hebrews, we'll discover together that we've only begun to scratch the surface of enjoying Jesus for who he is and what he has done. There is so much more. There is something better. Together, we'll discover . . .

There is something better than settling for a vague, diminished, distant understanding of who Jesus is, what he has done, and why it matters. It is seeing him more clearly and following him more closely.

There is something better than drifting along in a spiritual stream. It is grabbing hold of Jesus and drawing close.

There is something better than being enslaved to a debilitating dread of death. It is being set free by the promise of unending life.

There is something better than feeling like a hypocrite going through the motions of religion. It is an increasing intimacy with God and integrity with others.

There is something better than trying to work our way into God's good graces. It is resting in what Christ has done for us.

There is something better than staying on the fringes of an intimate relationship with God. It is boldly approaching him knowing we are accepted because of Jesus.

There is something better than continuing to go over the basics of faith. It is growing up in God by wrestling with deeper truths.

There is something better than trying to live up to an external standard of right and wrong. It is experiencing an internal transformation so that we want to do what is right.

There is something better than expecting to get everything we're hoping for here and now. It is a willingness to wait for all our deepest longings to be fulfilled in heaven.

There is something better than settling for the applause of people. It is anticipating the approval of God.

There is something better than the status of being an insider. It is the satisfaction of being connected to Christ even though we are rejected by the world.

There is something better than pursuing our own dreams of security and passion and significance. It is finding our security and passion and significance in God's dreams for us.

Let's refuse to settle for the Christian life as usual. Let's refuse to settle for anything less than something better.

before we get started

LAST WEEK A MAN who has written probably thirty Christian books told me that he has always seen Hebrews as a book for Jewish people, so he has never spent much time in it. And I had to tell him, "You're missing out on so much!" I couldn't help but share with him a few highlights from the truths I've discovered in my study of Hebrews that are for him and for me and for anyone else who wants to celebrate and enjoy all that Jesus means to those who place their faith in him.

I hope you've come to this book open to working the words of Hebrews into your life and will not depend solely on what I've written about it. I've created a resource in the back of this book so that you can study Hebrews by yourself or with a small group. To get the most out of the study, I suggest you work through the questions on the passage of Hebrews before reading the chapter on that particular passage. I suggest this for two reasons. First, as you work through the questions with your Bible open and your heart open to hear from God, he will speak to you through his Word, which is a thrilling and life-changing experience. Second, I think you will get more out of the chapter if you have already spent some time wrestling with the passage and its implications. Your familiarity with the passage and your lingering questions about what it means—and its implications for your life—will provide a foundation for you to respond to what the writer of Hebrews wants you to understand, accept, and do.

If you are studying the book of Hebrews with a group, I suggest that you meet first after reading the introduction to discuss what you have read, as well as what you hope to gain through this study. Prior to the next meeting, work through the questions on Hebrews 1:1–2:4 on your own and read chapter 1 of this book; then discuss as a group the questions as well as truths that have impacted you from the chapter. In this way you can work your way week by week through all ten chapters.

In the process of working on this book, whenever I told someone that I was working on a book about Hebrews, the response was often something like, "Wow, you're brave!" I'm not sure if I'm brave or just naive—or perhaps confident that God has something important to say to all of us in the challenging book of Hebrews. I know it was not written only for Bible scholars but for ordinary people like you and me.

I have found studying Hebrews to be so rich and so rewarding that I keep going back to it in my daily reading—going over the verses and chapters again and finding myself moved and challenged and changed all over again by its deep truths.

Don't be intimidated by the idea of studying Hebrews. I have no doubt that while some of the concepts and truths are challenging to grasp, they are worth persevering to understand and own. So open yourself to it, dive into it, chew on it, enjoy it, submit to it. And share it with each other.

And sometime along the way, go to my website at www.nancyguthrie.com and let me know how your study is going. I'd love to hear about it.

CHAPTER 1

what is God saying to you?

HEBREWS 1:1–2:4

My husband gave me a very thoughtful gift for my birthday last year. Since my birthday fell a week or so after Hurricane Katrina hit the Gulf Coast, he made a donation to the Salvation Army in my honor. I loved it! I didn't need anything or want anything else—and it fit just right!

But then he made a mistake. The morning after my birthday he showed me a catalog and said, "I was thinking about how you are teaching Hebrews this fall and that you might like something to carry your Bible and notes and notebook in, and I saw this bag but I wasn't sure if it was the right color or style or if you would like it, so I didn't get it."

Like it? I loved it! It was the season's color of green in suede and leather with a nickel buckle.

"You know, your mom sent me a check for my birthday that is the exact price of that bag," I told him, picturing myself with this oh-so-stylish tote hanging on my shoulder.

So the next day I sent him an e-mail:

From: Nancy Guthrie
Sent: Monday, September 12, 2005 10:42 a.m.
To: Guthrie, David
Subject: franklin covey bag
If you happen to be by the Franklin Covey place, I would love it if you would pick up that bag for me.
NG

And he e-mailed me back:

From: Guthrie, David
Sent: Monday, September 12, 2005 11:22 a.m.
To: Nancy Guthrie
Subject: RE: franklin covey bag
I was going to "happen to be there" shortly! Still likin' the green one?
DG

He brought it home that night. I wish you could see it. It is not too big and not too small. It has just the right mix of pockets on the inside, and it matches the green in several of my new fall outfits. I feel so chic.

Can you picture my bag in your mind as I tell you about it? Though you may have developed a picture of it in your mind, it is fuzzy and uncertain. Your mental picture will be slightly off in some way in terms of color or size or style.

So if I really want you to know what my new green bag looks like, I'll have to show it to you. If you could see the bag for yourself, then you would no longer have to settle for a picture of it in your mind that is slightly off. It would be clear.

In the same way, God wanted us to know exactly what he is like so we wouldn't have to be misguided or forever in the dark. So he went beyond describing himself and giving us pictures of what he is like. He has shown himself to us—in Jesus Christ. He went beyond words of description to giving us the living Word, the person of Jesus.

HOW DOES GOD SPEAK?

> *In the past God spoke to our forefathers through the prophets at many times and in various ways.* (HEBREWS 1:1)

From the first words of his sermon-letter, the writer to the Hebrews makes his case for showing these Jewish believers that the very purpose of everything in the Old Testament and their Temple traditions was to prepare them for the definitive revelation of God in the person of Christ.

Just as children are first taught letters, then words, and then sentences, God began revealing himself to us with the "picture book" of symbols and ceremonies. He started giving us a picture of who he is through the Law, the prophets, and the books of poetry—through the story of the children of Israel that was written down by more than forty writers over a 1,500-year time span. It was God speaking, but it was in bits and pieces, in forms and shadows. It wasn't wrong; it just wasn't complete.

> God has given us his written Word, the Bible, and his living Word, Jesus, and we need nothing further to know and follow God.

> *In these last days he has spoken to us by his Son, whom he appointed heir of all things, and through whom he made the universe.* (HEBREWS 1:2)

To the letter's recipients, "in these last days" didn't just mean "recently"; it referred to the anticipated messianic time. The Old Testament had said that "in the last days," the Messiah would come. But the phrase also means, in a sense, "finally." It is saying that God has been speaking in bits and pieces and now we have his final, complete, and authoritative Word. There is no fuller or more final expression of God than Jesus. Nothing further is needed; this is it.

And this is good for us to know, because many people today claim to have a word from God for us, and we are right to be skeptical or at least make sure it is confirmed by Scripture. Because Jesus himself is God's final and complete Word. God has given us his written Word, the Bible, and his living Word, Jesus, and we need nothing further to know and follow God.

God wants us to know what he is like, so he told us about himself. He began revealing himself to us in the Garden of Eden, as he showed us his love for beauty and order in his creation. He revealed the power of his wrath in the Flood and his ability to save in the ark. He revealed his ability to deliver us from captivity and bring us to the Promised Land in the story of the Israelites' escape from Egypt. He revealed his love for holiness and righteousness in the Law. He revealed his plan for the ages through the prophets. And he gave us some hints about how he was going to take care of our sin problem in the building of the Tabernacle and in the festivals, feasts, and sacrifices. He showed us his wisdom in Proverbs and his passion in Song of Songs. All of these gave us snapshots of what God is like and what he is doing in the world.

But our vision of God was still fuzzy and uncertain until . . . "the Word became flesh and dwelt among us, and we beheld His glory, the glory as of the only begotten of the Father, full of grace and truth" (John 1:14, NKJV).

In the person of Jesus, God has spoken and is still speaking into our lives.

Sometimes our feelings may tell us that God is silent. But when we complain that God is silent, when we're straining to hear the voice of God, what we are really saying is that we have exhausted this final decisive Word he has spoken to us in the person of Jesus and in the pages of Scripture. It's as if we are saying the Bible has nothing further to say to us, that we've seen all there is to see in Jesus and heard all there is to hear in the gospel, that it has no power to speak into our current situations.

But have we? Have we exhausted what Jesus has to say to us through his words and his ways and his work?

Or have we only given it a casual hearing, skimmed his Word like the newspaper and decided it simply doesn't apply or has no appeal?

WHAT IS GOD SAYING?

In Jesus, God is saying, "I want to show you who I am." We would never know God if he did not speak to us. And he wants us to know him for who he really is, not for who we want to make him to be. So many times we want to make him into a God who suits our liking. We hear people say, "Well, the God I believe in would never . . ." or "I believe God is . . ." almost as if we can determine what God is like merely by the whims of our own imaginations.

God doesn't need our help in designing his personality or deciding what he should be like. He is I AM, the eternal, self-existing one. And he wants us to see him and know him for who he really is.

One day when my son, Matt, was in early elementary school, he and I were driving along in the car discussing some lofty topic. I made the statement that we don't really know what Jesus looked like since we don't have a picture of him. Matt replied, "Yes we do. I've seen it."

Of course he was talking about the traditional painting of Jesus that we've all seen countless times and have come to think of as an actual rendering of the physical likeness of Jesus.

But while we don't have a photograph or a reliable painting of Jesus' outward appearance, Hebrews 1 paints a picture of the person of Jesus for those of us who want to see him and know him.

Jesus Is the Beloved Son (1:2)

In these last days he has spoken to us by his Son. (HEBREWS 1:2)

Larry King once said that if he could land an interview with God himself, he would have one question: "Did you have a son?"

I suppose that is because he knows that this has been the crucial question of history and religion. Was Jesus merely a good teacher and a prophet? Or was he the divine Son of God, the singular Savior?

Just this week I read a newspaper article about a church in which the pastor is "questioning the existence of a personal deity, and he says he doesn't believe Jesus is God." This is the pastor of the church. When I read this, I couldn't help but think to myself, *Then why bother with religion? Why bother with calling yourself by his name?*

> God himself has broken the silence of heaven to tell us that we need to listen to his beloved Son, Jesus.

Some religions diminish Jesus by calling him "a" son of God, suggesting that there have been others. But John describes Jesus as *the* Son of God, "the Father's one and only Son" (John 1:14, NLT).

Two of the significant times God spoke in an audible voice from heaven were when Jesus was baptized and when he was transfigured on the mountaintop. Both times he said for all to hear, "This is my Son, whom I love; with him I am well pleased" (Matthew 3:17). And at the Transfiguration he added, "Listen to him!" (Matthew 17:5). Jesus is loved and honored by his Father. God himself has broken the silence of heaven to tell us that we need to listen to his beloved Son, Jesus.

Jesus Is the Appointed Heir (1:2)

> *In these last days he has spoken to us by his Son, whom he appointed heir of all things.* (HEBREWS 1:2)

God, the creator and owner of this world, has chosen Jesus to inherit everything. It's all his. So what does this mean in practical terms? This means that Jesus, the Son of God, can make good on all that he has promised to give us. Why? Because he has all the resources. He is the heir of all things.

Romans 11:36 says that "from him and through him and to him are all things." Everything that exists, exists for Jesus.

In the end Jesus will have under his complete control and ownership all things—all natural resources, all governmental power, all human intelligence, all the riches of the earth. Everything will be at his disposal and command.

And while Jesus doesn't have to split the inheritance, he will.

My parents recently bought the house next door to my brother. He has been the "in-town" child living near my parents for years while my sister and I have lived in other cities, and he has enjoyed telling my sister and me that because of the heavier load he has carried for parental care, when the inheritance comes, it is not going to be split evenly three ways. (I think he's kidding. You are kidding, right, Tom?)

While Tom may kid me about being stingy with our inheritance, I've been adopted into another family. And I know my brother, Jesus, will not keep his inheritance to himself. Jesus has promised that he will share all that he inherits. In Romans 8:16-17 we read that "the Spirit himself testifies with our spirit that we are God's children. Now if we are children, then we are heirs—heirs of God and co-heirs with Christ."

Have you ever heard the Spirit of God whispering to your own spirit that you are his child? If so, then one day Jesus will share with you all that he possesses. In fact, Jesus is so generous, he offers to share his inheritance with anyone who will trust in him.

Jesus Is the Universe Creator (1:2)

> *In these last days he has spoken to us by his Son . . . through whom he made the universe.* (HEBREWS 1:2)

You might have thought that God the Father created the heavens and the earth and that Jesus did not appear on the scene until he was born in Bethlehem. But Jesus was with God the Father as the Living Word from eternity past. While God the Father is the source of all creation, it was Jesus, his creative agent, the Living Word, who called creation into being.

Jesus has the ability to create something out of nothing. John 1:3 says that "all things came into being through Him, and apart from Him nothing came into being that has come into being" (NASB).

But the word in Hebrews 1:2 for what he has created is not *kosmos,* which refers to the physical universe. It is a word that is translated "the ages." So Jesus not only created the physical earth, he created time, space, energy, and matter—all without effort—just by speaking it into being.[1]

When we look through a telescope at amazing outer galaxies or when we touch the delicate finger of a tiny baby, we don't have to wonder where it all came from. As we welcome the changing of the seasons or study the rise and fall of empires throughout history, we recognize that it is Jesus who set it all in motion. The Bible tells us the maker of all things is Jesus Christ.

Jesus Is the Radiant Glory (1:3)

> *The Son is the radiance of God's glory.* (HEBREWS 1:3)

We see the sun by means of seeing the rays of the sun. They are the essence of the sun flowing out of the sun. The round ball of fire that we see in the sky is the sun streaming forth in its radiance. To say that Jesus is the radiance of God's glory is to say that Jesus relates to God the way the rays of sunlight relate to the sun. We see God the Father by seeing Jesus. Jesus is the radiance of God streaming down on us so we can see him and experience him and know him.

Jesus is the radiance of God streaming down on us so we can see him and experience him and know him.

The term "God's glory" had deeper meaning for the original Hebrew recipients of this letter than it does for us today. These Hebrews remembered hearing about the glory cloud of God's presence that lit the sky and led the children of Israel in the desert. It was the tangible presence of God in their midst. And now the writer of Hebrews is saying that Jesus is the ultimate cloud of glory. In fact, Jesus is the fire of God's glory that will not burn or consume us. Jesus enables us to relate to the glory of God in human form.

Standing in the Temple one day, Jesus said, "I am the light of the world. Whoever follows me will never walk in darkness, but will have the light of life" (John 8:12). We live in a dark world, and perhaps there are circumstances in your life right now that would cause you to say that your world is very dark. Into the darkness of this world God sent his Son, Jesus, so that we could see and live in the radiance of his glory. Even now, Jesus is the only sure source of light for the dark places in our lives. He brings the radiant light of God's presence into our darkness.

Jesus is God's full personality and power and purpose in a person. He's a precise copy, a perfect imprint, an exact reproduction; he is no less than God himself in human form.

Jesus Is the Exact Representation (1:3)

The Son is . . . the exact representation of his being.
(Hebrews 1:3)

Did you ever have one of those Hallmark sets for sealing envelopes? I had one in grade school. I would light the candle and melt the wax onto my stylish stationery envelope and then press onto the wax a big metal seal with an *N* and hold it until the wax hardened. When I pulled away the metal seal, a perfect *N*, an exact representation of the metal seal, was left in the hardened wax.

Jesus is the perfect, personal imprint of God in time and space. As Colossians 1:15 says, "He is the image of the invisible God."

Some people see the God of the Old Testament and Jesus of the New Testament as two dramatically different beings—

a sort of good-cop/bad-cop scenario. They like the gentle, nonjudgmental Jesus on the hillside teaching and healing, but they reject the vengeful God of judgment they've picked up from selected Old Testament stories.

But Jesus is not the softer side of God. Jesus is God's full personality and power and purpose in a person. He's a precise copy, a perfect imprint, an exact reproduction; he is no less than God himself in human form.

Jesus Is the Powerful Sustainer (1:3)

The Son . . . sustain[s] all things by his powerful word. (HEBREWS 1:3)

Everything in the universe is sustained right now by Jesus. Imagine if the sustainer suspended the law of gravity for just a few moments. Imagine if the sustainer tilted the axis of the earth a few degrees. Jesus didn't just make the world and leave it on its own. The reason there is order to the seasons and the sun keeps coming up in the morning is because Jesus Christ is the powerful sustainer.

But understanding Jesus as the sustainer is not just about his holding the physical world in place; it is more about Jesus' governance and authority and direction of history. Jesus oversees the progression of time, the course of history. And he does so by the power of his word. No further effort required.

Think about the implications of this. Jesus sustains everything in this universe with the power of his word. And you are on the fence trying to decide if Jesus is up to your standards? You wonder if he is strong enough to take on your situation? You doubt that Jesus is smart enough to deal effectively with your doubts and questions? You question if you can trust him with your life?

Whenever you wonder where this world is headed or if it is spinning out of control, you can rest in the confidence that Jesus is sustaining all things by the power of his word. Nothing happens by accident in this world. He says so, and it is done. The "all things" he is sustaining includes you and those you love. He is strong enough and sovereign enough not only to guide this universe into fulfilling its destiny but also to bring you into the fullness of all he has for you in himself. As it says in Philippians 1:6, "He who began a good work in you will carry it on to completion." Jesus is the powerful Sustainer—sustaining you, upholding you, completing you.

Jesus Is the Sin Purifier (1:3)

After he had provided purification for sins, he sat down at the right hand of the Majesty in heaven. (HEBREWS 1:3)

Do you remember watching the television coverage of Hurricane Katrina? I found that I plugged my nose from the inside while I watched, because I imagined I could smell the stench through the TV screen. Looking at the sludge-filled homes and trashed neighborhoods, I couldn't help but wonder, *How will it ever become clean again?*

Likewise, when the radiance of God's glory shines into our lives and reveals what is there, and we see ourselves for who we really are, we can't help but wonder, *How can I ever become clean again?* It seems impossible. We wonder how we'll ever get rid of the stains of our past failures—the blot of divorce, the ugliness of cruelty, the emotional debris left behind by sex outside of marriage, the filth of what we've let our eyes see, the contamination of the words that have passed across our lips, the corruption of our selfish motives, the utter apathy in our hearts toward God. We realize that we are utterly ruined by sin.

> Jesus is the sin purifier. His blood is the only cleanser that will take away the stains sin has left in our lives.

And while that may sound miserable—and it is—it is the best thing that can happen to us. It is when we realize that we are ruined, that we can't clean up our act ourselves, that we recognize, perhaps for the first time, how relevant Jesus is. Jesus is the sin purifier. His blood is the only cleanser that will take away the stains sin has left in our lives.

And I have to wonder, if that doesn't mean something to you, have you really seen yourself the way God sees you? We tend to compare ourselves to other people and think we look pretty good. But when we see ourselves the way God sees us—in contrast to the beauty and perfection of Christ—we see ourselves as we truly are: covered and contaminated by sin, inundated with dark thoughts of God, and plagued by indifference toward God—perhaps the ugliest sin of all.

Have you ever realized that you are ruined by sin, desperately in need of the sin purifier? Have you ever asked the sin purifier to come into your life and clean up the mess you have made?

We don't have to get our lives cleaned up before we give ourselves to Jesus. That is like cleaning up the house before the maid gets there. We can come to him as we are, and he will take away the ugliness of our sin and give us his own perfect righteousness. This is the gift that makes it possible for us to one day enter the very presence of God.

You see, no one goes to heaven because he or she has been good. Who could ever be good enough to enter the presence of a holy God? No one. What you and I desperately need in order to have any hope of living forever in the pure presence of God is to be cleansed by the sin purifier—to trade in our sin-stained record, sin-plagued thoughts and motives, and even our own spot-ridden righteousness, for the righteousness of Christ, the perfection he offers to us as a gift.

He will give you his own righteousness if you ask him to, but he doesn't rush into your life uninvited. Have you ever invited the sin purifier to cleanse you and cover you with his perfect righteousness?

Jesus Is the Seated Ruler (1:3)

He sat down at the right hand of the Majesty in heaven. (HEBREWS 1:3)

I've found it is impossible to take a nap when I have a long to-do list running through my mind. I can't really rest because there is work to be done. But when the work is done, I can rest.

There were no seats in the Old Testament Temple as God designed it. None were needed because the priests could never sit down. Their work was never done. It was day after day, year after year, making sacrifices to cover sin, never finished until . . .

Until that day when Jesus uttered his final words as he hung on the cross. Do you remember what he said? "It is finished." What was finished? The work he had come to do—the giving of himself as the perfect, once-for-all sacrifice for sin. He finished the work. And now that the work has been completed, he is seated.

> Jesus is seated at the right hand of God, telling him what you need when you don't even have the words for it or the will to ask for it.

Did you really hear that? The work is done. The work

required for us to come into the presence of God has been completed by Jesus. Not only is he now resting, but we can rest too. We can stop trying so hard to work for God or work our way to God. The work has been completed by Jesus on our behalf. We can rest.

But this verse doesn't just speak to Jesus being seated; it tells us *where* he is seated. Jesus is seated at the right hand of God the Father, the place of honor and usefulness, power and authority.

Romans 8:34 says that Jesus is "at the right hand of God and is also interceding for us." Jesus is seated at the right hand of the Father, making intercession for those who belong to him. Jesus is seated at the right hand of God, telling him what you need when you don't even have the words for it or the will to ask for it.

Jesus Is the Angels' Authority (1:4-7)

> *He became as much superior to the angels as the name he has inherited is superior to theirs.* (HEBREWS 1:4)

The Hebrews who originally received this letter saw angels as the ones who delivered the Ten Commandments, so they recognized that angels have power and authority. But some of these early believers were confused about where Jesus fit in with the angels. They wanted to see an organizational chart so they could understand the chain of command. This writer made it clear that Jesus is the one the angels worship and obey. Angels are created beings, but Jesus is the Son. While angels do God's bidding, God has exalted the Son, and the angels serve him.

People today love the idea of angels. I think it is because angels offer spirituality with no demands, a touch of the supernatural without any kind of commitment on our part.

I get letters from many people who have lost loved ones. So often these hurting people find comfort in the idea that the person who has died is "now an angel in heaven watching over me."

In fact, as I was studying this first chapter of Hebrews I received a letter from a woman who had lost a child. She also sent me the manuscript for a sweet and beautiful book she had written for children on the loss of a sibling, in which an angel showed the child around heaven. She was asking for my advice and endorsement, and I found it very hard to know how to respond. Here's what I wrote to her, in part:

> Your letter with your children's book manuscript arrived at an interesting time. I am diligently studying the book of Hebrews. The writer of this letter to the Hebrews knew that the people of that day found it easier somehow to worship angels than to worship Jesus.
>
> I think your book is very sweet, and I know your heart is to create a resource that will take some of the sting of death from children who have to experience it, which is a worthy goal. But I think it is very important to comfort children and each other with the truth, and the best source of truth is the Scriptures. So we have to be very careful that what we write is faithful to the teachings of Scripture.
>
> I have a hard time with the strong emphasis on angels at the expense of a focus on Jesus in the book. It is Jesus who will make heaven all that it will be, and I think we do a disservice to adults and to children if we take the more sentimental route of a focus on angels and diminish Jesus in the process. I can't help but believe that if our children had any message to send us from heaven it would be, "Jesus is beautiful! Jesus is everything! Jesus is worth waiting for!"
>
> Angels are important. God created them, and they serve an important function in this world in service to God and to his saints. But people do not become angels when they die. Babies do not become angels. They're better than that. They are God's beloved children who rest safe in his arms. And while we might find it comforting to think about them watching over us, if we really think about that, do we want them to have that kind of sorrow and responsibility? Or do we just want them to enjoy Jesus and enjoy a perfected body, a perfected mind, and perfected emotions . . . complete perfection?

Angels are ministers and messengers. People are quick to credit their "guardian angel" when they feel they've been supernaturally taken care of, and certainly Hebrews 1:14 tells us that angels are sent to serve the saints. But angels don't initiate this service on their own. They're sent. And shouldn't the real credit go to the one who sent the angel?

I suppose the question of angels comes down to this: Why settle for the servants when you can know the Son? Jesus, the Son, is served by the angels of heaven, and he is the one who sends angels to serve us.

Jesus Is the Enemy Defeater (1:13)

> *To which of the angels did God ever say, "Sit at my right hand until I make your enemies a footstool for your feet"?* (HEBREWS 1:13)

Do you sometimes look around at the world and wonder where it is headed? Doesn't it sometimes seem like it is in a steady spiral downward—morally, politically, and socially?

When you see looters walking off with television sets and murderers who are set free on technicalities and corrupt corporate officers who make off with workers' pension funds, don't you long for someone to make things right? Don't you long for evil to be punished?

Evil *will* be punished, my friend. The enemies of God—those who have rejected him and rebelled against him—will one day experience the wrath of God. They will get what is coming to them. You can rest in that. You can surrender your right to revenge because of that. "'It is mine to avenge; I will repay,' says the Lord" (Romans 12:19). Jesus' defeat of his enemies is sure and certain.

And if you have been God's enemy until now, you can become his friend. We all start out as enemies of God. Romans 5:10 says, "For if, when we were God's enemies, we were reconciled to him through the death of his Son, how much more, having been reconciled, shall we be saved through his life!" This is how good Jesus is. He has extended himself in love so that his enemies can become his friends.

Are you starting to see Jesus a little more clearly now in your mind's eye?

So many people want to reduce Jesus to a great moral teacher. They want to pick and choose what appeals to them about what he said and what he did.

But Jesus is the transcendent God of the universe. If you find yourself struggling to wrap your brain and heart around all that Jesus is, you're beginning to see him for who he really is.

If you find yourself struggling to wrap your brain and heart around all that Jesus is, you're beginning to see him for who he really is.

If all of this is true about Jesus, can you see that you must give your life to him—and keep giving your life to him?

Honestly, most people don't see that. Most people in this world live with a vague sense of who Jesus is and no acknowledgment of the need to respond to him. But when we see Jesus for who he really is, how can anyone reduce Jesus to a "take it or leave it" religious option? How could we assume that we can be neutral about him or take bits and pieces of him, or ignore him?

Jesus is worthy of our worship.

Jesus is worthy of our very lives.

HOW CAN WE KNOW WHAT GOD IS SAYING IS TRUE?

> *This salvation, which was first announced by the Lord, was confirmed to us by those who heard him. God also testified to it by signs, wonders and various miracles, and gifts of the Holy Spirit distributed according to his will.* (Hebrews 2:3-4)

If we're going to be intellectually honest, we have to ask and answer the question, How can we know that what this writer to the Hebrews is saying about Jesus is true?

Spoken by Jesus

For one thing, what the writer of Hebrews wrote about Jesus is compatible with what Jesus said about himself. Over and over again, Jesus made it clear that he is the only Son of the Father in heaven, that God has entrusted all things to him, that seeing him is seeing the Father, and that he has the power to forgive and cleanse sin.

Jesus was clear that he is the source of salvation and that there is no other. We receive that salvation by grace through faith in Jesus.

WHAT JESUS SAID ABOUT HIMSELF

"For God so loved the world that he gave his one and only Son" (John 3:16). Jesus is the beloved Son.

"All that belongs to the Father is mine" (John 16:15). Jesus is the appointed heir.

"Now is the Son of Man glorified and God is glorified in him" (John 13:31). Jesus is the radiant glory.

"Anyone who has seen me has seen the Father" (John 14:9). Jesus is the exact representation.

"I am the living bread that came down from heaven. If anyone eats of this bread, he will live forever" (John 6:51). Jesus is the powerful sustainer.

"Take heart, son; your sins are forgiven" (Matthew 9:2). Jesus is the sin purifier.

Confirmed by Witnesses

In addition to Jesus' own words, Jesus' words and actions were confirmed by those who witnessed his person and his power.

The second-generation believers reading this original letter hadn't heard Jesus speak with their own ears. They hadn't heard him on the hillside teaching. They hadn't seen him on the cross dying. But people who were there, who did hear and see, confirmed these events in the Gospels and the other pages of the New Testament, making it a reliable record.

Validated by Signs

Along with telling people he was the Son of God, Jesus did some things that made his words impossible not to believe. He said, "Though you do not believe Me, believe the works, that you may know and believe that the Father is in Me, and I in Him" (John 10:38, NKJV). Jesus claimed to be God, and then he did things only God could do. He walked on water and healed the sick; he knew people's inner thoughts and motives. He lived a life uncorrupted by sin.

His disciples were also able to do things that only God could empower them to do. God gave them the ability to raise the dead and heal diseases. This was God's way of giving them credibility, so that people would believe what they said about who Jesus was and how to be saved.

WHAT WILL YOU DO WITH WHAT GOD HAS SAID?

God has spoken eloquently—on his own terms, in his own way, in his own time. But are you really listening? How can you experience what God is saying?

Pay Close Attention (2:1)

> *We must pay more careful attention, therefore, to what we have heard, so that we do not drift away.* (HEBREWS 2:1)

Tim Keller has said that this instruction to "pay more careful attention" could more accurately be rendered as "be furiously obsessed with."[2] The writer is saying that unless we remain furiously obsessed with the original message of the gospel, we are going to drift. We can get sidetracked by the latest fads in religious thinking, the latest best-selling book, the newest "it" teacher. So we have to stay focused on the person and work of Christ, on who Scripture reveals him to be. We can never exhaust the Word's meaning or implications in our lives.

> We have to stay focused on the person and work of Christ, on who Scripture reveals him to be. We can never exhaust the Word's meaning or implications in our lives.

When we want to pay close attention to something, we clear away distractions; we set aside the time and space so that we can listen. We make plans and provisions to listen. If we want to listen to music, we buy a car with a CD player and we put CDs in the car. If we want to hear from family and friends, we exchange phone numbers or set up Internet access to our homes so we can call or e-mail each other.

What provisions have you made so that you can pay close attention to what God has said in his written Word and in his living Word—Jesus? Have you determined when during your day and during your week you will set aside time to study God's Word so that you can pay close attention to what he is saying to you through this study of Hebrews? Are you willing to leave behind a casual approach to listening to what God has to say to you, or does a new level of accountability make you uncomfortable and uneasy?

Do you find yourself too sophisticated, too busy with "important" things to be "furiously obsessed" with Jesus? If not, what provisions and plans are you willing to make so that you can pay close attention to Jesus?

Don't Drift Away (2:1)

It doesn't take any effort to drift. If you've ever gotten on an air mattress and floated down a river on a sunny day, you know that there is real pleasure in drifting—at least for a while. But it doesn't necessarily take you where you want to go.

We have been invited to tie up our air mattresses to the safe and secure harbor of salvation. But some of us have just never made that commitment. We haven't tied ourselves to Jesus. And we're in danger of drifting. We may be interested in Christ and intend to stay close, but time and circumstances cause us to drift, and without even realizing it, we may find ourselves slipping away completely from the opportunity to know Jesus in a saving way.[3]

Others of us have tethered ourselves to Christ, and yet in our hearts and minds we are drifting. If you're honest, would you have to say that as you look back over your life, there was a time you were more in love with Jesus, more fascinated with his Word, more attuned to his Spirit than you are now? Was there a time you were closer to Jesus? You never made a decision to drift away. You never intended for the relationship to grow cold. But you've drifted. You've lost that firm grip.

This word of warning is for all of us: We need to nurture our furious obsessions with Jesus. Let's anchor ourselves to him, stay close to him, and not allow ourselves to drift.

Don't Neglect Salvation (2:3)

How shall we escape if we ignore such a great salvation? (Hebrews 2:3)

One Sunday I got to church, and in the middle of the service I realized something embarrassing. I had forgotten to put on any makeup. I must have planned to do it after breakfast and then just forgot in the rush of getting out the door. Even though my husband assures me that I'm "one of those women" who looks good without makeup, I was horrified.

Some of you natural beauties may think that is silly—but others of you are horrified with me. You would never show up in public without washing your hair or putting on your makeup. Others of you would be horrified at the thought of neglecting your yard. You would never let the grass go to seed and the weeds overtake the flower beds.

You would never neglect your family, never fail to buy needed food or provide clothes for your children or get involved in their education. You would never neglect your business, never fail to return phone calls and e-mails or follow through on projects.

And yet some of us can be completely comfortable neglecting our salvation. We just take it for granted.

But what is interesting and unexpected in this passage is that the writer is not telling us here to get to work. What he's really saying is don't neglect being loved by God. Don't neglect being forgiven and accepted and protected and strengthened and guided by almighty God. Don't neglect the sacrifice of Christ's death on the cross. Don't neglect seeing the radiance of God's glory in the face of Jesus. Don't neglect enjoying the free access to the throne of grace. Don't neglect the inexhaustible treasure of God's promises. This is a great salvation. Don't neglect so great a salvation.[4] It is the something better you've been hoping for.

Remember my green bag?

I could have just looked at the picture of the green bag and said, "That's a nice bag. It would be nice to have a bag like that. Someday I'll get myself a bag like that."

That's what many people do in regard to Jesus. They think that maybe someday they will get around to getting Jesus. And somehow they never get around to it. There is this

God has spoken to us plainly, clearly, personally in the person and work of Jesus. And we need no other word. Jesus is everything God wants to say to us.

incredible salvation available to them, and they neglect it. They never claim it for themselves.

I also could have bought the bag and then just put it on the shelf for someday when I needed it, never making it part of my life. What a shame, to put Jesus on the shelf, never making him a part of our day-to-day lives.

God's message to us in Jesus requires a response. God has spoken to us plainly, clearly, personally in the person and work of Jesus. And we need no other word. Jesus is everything God wants to say to us.

Are you listening?

Jesus is everything God wants to say to us.

CHAPTER 2

what are you afraid of?

HEBREWS 2:5-18

DON'T GET MY HUSBAND started. That is, don't get him started telling his funeral home stories unless you really want to hear them, because he can go on for hours. The college David attended had a policy that all students must live on campus unless their job required them to live elsewhere. And since David didn't like living by the rules on campus, he was thrilled when an opening came up to work at the nearby funeral home, which meant living at the funeral home and answering phones during the night.

I must admit, he's got some good stories—the Hell's Angels funeral is a good one, and the story about transporting a body across the state line without the proper paperwork is good, and of course the stories of getting spooked by sounds in the middle of the night are crowd pleasers.

But for most of us, the subject of death is not high on our dinner party conversation list. For some of us, this is a subject that hits too close to home. It is a topic that brings pain and arouses fear.

When David and I brought our daughter, Hope, home from the hospital a week after she was born, it wasn't at all the homecoming I had anticipated it would be. I knew we were bringing her home to die.

Hope was born with a rare metabolic disorder, and the doctor who diagnosed it on her second day of life told us to expect to have her for two to three months. It wasn't long after we brought her home that the fear began to set in. I realized that her death was not a way-out-there possibility at some time in the distant future. It was a certainty, and it would likely be soon. I realized that either she would die in my arms or I would go to her crib and find her dead, and that bitter reality took my breath away.

The truth is, it is only after we wrangle with our fear of death and put death in its proper place that we can really begin to live.

I was afraid—afraid of what her death would be like. Would she suffer? I was afraid of what it would be like to hold her dead body. Would that become my most vivid memory of her? And I was afraid of what grief would be like, of what it would do to me, of the person it would make me.

If I tell you that in this chapter we're going to talk about death, does that sound like a bummer to you? The truth is, it is only after we wrangle with our fear of death and put death in its proper place that we can really begin to live. And we want to really live, don't we? Isn't that an important part of the "something better" we've been hoping for?

Most of the world lives in major denial about death—with the illusion that if they don't think about it, it won't happen, and with the superstition that if they dare to discuss it, it is doomed to happen. They don't want to talk about death or do much preparing for it in an attempt to keep it at bay.

We have a hard time imagining how or why anyone could do anything—even for a noble cause, such as defending one's country, donating a vital organ, or running into a burning building—that could potentially lead to death. Why anyone would choose to forgo an invasive medical treatment that might add days or months to his or her life on this earth is a mystery to many of us. So we wear our seat belts and take our vitamins and invest in new technologies—whatever it takes to keep death at a distance.

If we think about it, can't we trace the root of nearly every fear we experience to our fear of death? What are we so afraid of?

I think we're afraid of what is unknown about death. We fear the pain of death and the pain our death will cause to others. We fear the separation that is inherent in death. We fear the loss of control that death and dying bring. We fear the finality of death. Many of us fear the judgment that will follow death.

The thing about death is, no matter how old the person is who dies, no matter the cause of his or her death, no matter how many times someone tells us that death is perfectly natural, something deep inside us cries out, *This is not right. This is not how it is supposed to be.*

And that voice is the voice of truth. We were never meant to die. Death was not a part of our original destiny.

So what was our original destiny?

THE REASON FOR OUR FEAR

Our Original Destiny (2:5-8)

> *It is not to angels that he has subjected the world to come, about which we are speaking.* (HEBREWS 2:5)

Continuing his argument from Hebrews 1 about the role and responsibility of angels, the writer to the Hebrews states that angels are not going to rule the world to come. God's ultimate intention was and is to have his Kingdom ruled by redeemed men and women. He builds his argument for this by quoting Psalm 8:

> *But there is a place where someone has testified: "What is man that you are mindful of him, the son of man that you care for him? You made him a little lower than the angels; you crowned him with glory and honor and put everything under his feet."* (HEBREWS 2:6-8)

Psalm 8 contemplates the expanse of the sky and wonders at God's intention for puny little humans. The psalmist is celebrating the creation of the world by God described in Genesis:

Then God said, "Let us make man in our image, in our likeness, and let them rule over the fish of the sea and the birds of the air, over the livestock, over all the earth, and over all the creatures that move along the ground." So God created man in his own image, in the image of God he created him; male and female he created them. God blessed them and said to them, "Be fruitful and increase in number; fill the earth and subdue it. Rule over the fish of the sea and the birds of the air and over every living creature that moves on the ground." (GENESIS 1:26-28)

In Genesis we see that God made the world and gave it to us to cultivate and nurture. He put us in charge and made us responsible for it. Hebrews 2:8, quoting Psalm 8, says that God put everything under the subjection of people. By quoting this psalm, the writer to the Hebrews is reminding these believers of God's ultimate plan: for redeemed men and women to rule the earth and subdue it.

But then, almost as if he anticipates that someone in the crowd is going to speak up and say, "Yeah, but . . . have you taken a look around lately?" the writer to the Hebrews goes on to offer a sort of disclaimer in verse 8.

The Difficult Reality (2:8)

Yet at present we do not see everything subject to him. (HEBREWS 2:8)

Obviously, the world is not in complete subjection to man. We're supposed to be ruling, but the reality is, we are subject to this cursed creation in dreadful ways. Rather than ruling the animals, we're susceptible to West Nile virus–carrying mosquitoes and the bird flu. Rather than subduing the earth, we neglect and abuse it. We're vulnerable to its hurricanes and heat waves. Rather than being fruitful, we find ourselves living in futility.

Sin ruined everything, and everything changed. Nothing is the way it was created to be.

When Adam and Eve sinned, they immediately lost their kingdom and their crowns. They became slaves to sin. When sin entered this perfect world, it wasn't only humans who felt the effects. All of creation became cursed. The animal kingdom was no longer tame, the ground became full of thorns and weeds, and the atmosphere produced deadly weather extremes.

Remember the warning of Genesis 2:17? "Of the tree of the knowledge of good and evil you shall not eat, for in the day that you eat of it you shall surely die" (NKJV). God doesn't make false threats, and this was no exception. Sin brought death.

The ultimate curse of our lost destiny is death. And death doesn't play favorites. One hundred percent of humans die. We can't earn enough, know enough, or stay healthy enough, powerful enough, or technologically sophisticated enough to overcome death. We try. We go on diets. We buy expensive creams and dream of our own "extreme makeovers." We search for cures for our diseases and ride our exercise bicycles and eat our vegetables. But we all die.

> Jesus came so that the fear of death would not have to rule our emotions or dominate our thoughts.

It was into this difficult reality of rampant death that Jesus came. He said, "I have come that they may have life, and have it to the full" (John 10:10). Jesus came so that the fear of death would not have to rule our emotions or dominate our thoughts.

We do not have to face our own deaths or the deaths of those we love gripped by fear and dread. We will grieve. When we lose something or someone who is valuable to us, we're sad, and there is nothing wrong with that. But because of Jesus, we can face our own deaths or the deaths of those we love with peace and confidence and rest.

THE SOLUTION TO OUR FEAR

Hebrews tells us why and how we can face death without being a slave to fear:

> *At present we do not see everything subject to him. But we see Jesus.*
> (HEBREWS 2:8-9)

Seeing Jesus gives us hope for reclaiming the destiny that was lost, because Jesus has reclaimed it for us. Seeing Jesus helps us deal with the difficult reality of living in this in-between time, when death is a constant companion. The rest of Hebrews 2 helps us see clearly what it is about Jesus that provides the solution to our debilitating fear of death. This chapter holds a magnifying glass up to our Savior so we can see and no longer be so afraid.

Jesus Fulfilled Our Destiny (2:6, 9)

Psalm 8 is not only a celebration of the magnificent destiny of man. It is also a messianic psalm that has its ultimate fulfillment in the ultimate man: Christ.

> *What is man that you are mindful of him, the son of man that you care for him?* (HEBREWS 2:6)

Do you remember how Jesus often referred to himself as "the Son of Man"? Jesus is the ultimate, perfect Son of Man. He fulfills everything Psalm 8 celebrates regarding humanity. When we read that this Son of Man is "crowned with glory and honor" and that God put "everything under his feet," we recognize immediately that Psalm 8 is not true of us. But it is true of Jesus, and through Jesus, as we unite ourselves with him, it will be true of us. It is through our identification with Christ, our oneness with Christ, that we also fulfill the destiny originally designed for us and revealed to us in Psalm 8.

> *We see Jesus, who was made a little lower than the angels, now crowned with glory and honor because he suffered death.* (HEBREWS 2:9)

Jesus endured suffering and death, and now he is crowned with glory and honor. He is seated in power at the right hand of God, and all his enemies are subjected to him as a footstool for his feet. In the reality beyond this world that we cannot see with our physical eyes but by faith choose to gaze upon with spiritual eyes, Jesus is seated on the throne, ruling this world. Don't you wish we could see this reality now?

When we see deadly tsunamis and hurricanes and earthquakes around the world, we can't help but wonder, *God, are you on the throne?* As terrorism increases and the ozone layer decreases, as world economies rise and fall, we strain to keep believing that God is on the throne. When the doctor calls with a dreaded diagnosis or when your husband walks out on you or when the bill collectors keep calling, a voice cries out inside saying, *God, are you on the throne?*

It is in these times that, even though we can't see him on the throne with our physical eyes, we see through eyes of faith. And we long for the day when we get to see Jesus on the throne, when we get to see what his glory looks like with our eyes and see all his enemies—enemies like crime and cruelty and disease and dishonesty and death—crushed beneath his feet. This is what it means for our faith to become sight.

But what is even more amazing and inviting is the promise that Jesus does not intend to keep this glory of ruling on the throne to himself. Verse 10 says that he is "bringing many sons to glory"—the glory described in Psalm 8. United with Jesus, we, too, will experience the fulfillment of Psalm 8. We, too, will enjoy the joy and beauty and perfection of one day being in the presence of God because of our connection to Jesus.

But there is still a dose of reality for us in this. Psalm 8 says, "You crowned him with glory and honor and put everything under his feet." If we're honest, we have to say that it doesn't really seem like Jesus has made a footstool of his enemies. It often seems like evil is winning in this world, doesn't it? Christ does not seem to be in complete control. Or if he is, he sure is letting evil in this world get away with a lot.

That is because we are living in an in-between time. Jesus has established his Kingdom, and its effects have been set into motion, but the full realization of Jesus' reign and his removal of all evil have been postponed until he returns to earth for that very purpose. So we now live in this in-between time that is marked by tears and pain and death.

We now live in this in-between time that is marked by tears and pain and death.

But a day is coming when our tears will be wiped away—when there will be no more sorrow, no more pain, no more death. We will not always live in this in-between time. That hope waiting for us out in the future—the ultimate something better, secured for us by Jesus—helps us now as we live in the pain of the present.

To the extent that we see Jesus and place our faith in him, we can say, "Psalm 8 is my destiny. Because I am in Christ, all things will one day be put under my feet. I will rule with him in glory forever and ever."[5]

Our final destiny is not the grave. Our final destiny is glory. Jesus has blazed the trail ahead of us. He has gone into the future and secured it for us—a world the way it is supposed to be.

Jesus Tasted Our Death (2:9)

By the grace of God he might taste death for everyone. (HEBREWS 2:9)

While it may be easy to see Jesus' death as a beautiful and inspiring example of dying for a cause, it can be hard to accept that he did it to take our place. But that is the astonishing truth of the gospel that we can grasp only through faith.

We see Jesus and we believe he is the fulfillment of Isaiah 53:5, which prophesied that the Messiah was "wounded for our transgressions; he was crushed for our iniquities; upon him was the chastisement that brought us peace, and with his stripes we are healed" (ESV). All the punishment for every sin—all the sin commited by those God calls as his own—was all laid on Jesus.

Jesus tasted death as our substitute so we don't have to.

Jesus drank the cup of wrath for us for every cruel word, every spiteful action, every selfish grab, every sexual indiscretion, every prideful attitude. And because he drank it as our substitute, we don't have to.

There is a phenomenon at our house that may sound familiar to you. It never fails. Someone drinks some milk and determines that it has gone sour, and then he looks at me and says, "This milk is bad. Here, taste it."

Why does he want me to taste it? I'll take his word for it! Why should I take a swig of sour milk if I don't have to, if someone has tasted it for me?

Mark 14:36 describes Jesus praying in the garden of Gethsemane. "Take this cup from me. Yet not what I will, but what you will." What cup is he talking about? The cup of God's wrath. The cup of the punishment of death for sin.

Because it was God's will and the very purpose for which Jesus came to earth, he said, "I'll drink it." Jesus drank the cup of God's wrath that we deserve so we don't have to. Jesus drank the cup of wrath for us for every cruel word, every spiteful action, every selfish grab, every sexual indiscretion, every prideful attitude. And because he drank it as our substitute, we don't have to.

Jesus experienced the judgment, the pain, the separation, the unknowns of death so we don't have to. That means we don't have to be afraid of physical death. It is merely our passageway to life. Jesus tasted eternal death as our substitute so we can experience eternal life.

Jesus Entered Our Reality (2:10-18)

> *In bringing many sons to glory, it was fitting that God, for whom and through whom everything exists, should make the author of their salvation perfect through suffering.* (HEBREWS 2:10)

In Hebrews 1, we saw Jesus in his full deity—in his power and glory as the beloved Son, appointed heir, radiant glory, exact imprint, universe creator, powerful sustainer, sin purifier, and seated ruler.

But Jesus is not only fully divine. In a holy mystery we can't completely comprehend or explain, Jesus is at once fully divine and fully human. In Hebrews 2, we see Jesus in his humanity, lowering himself, getting involved, sharing with us, living with us, becoming one of us.

Jews had difficulty with the whole concept of a God who would lower himself to suffer. It just didn't seem very godlike to them.

So when the writer to the Hebrews says, "It was fitting that God, for whom and through whom everything exists, should make the author of their salvation perfect through suffering," it means that what God did through Jesus is consistent with God's character. The author is challenging the conventional parameters for what is godlike. It is as if he points to the Cross and says, "This is not shameful. This is beautiful. It is appropriate and consistent with who God is."

He endured the reality of our suffering (2:10)

> *It was fitting that God . . . should make the author of their salvation perfect through suffering.* (HEBREWS 2:10)

The writer of Hebrews is telling us that suffering was not unbecoming to our Savior; it in fact produced a perfected Savior. In what way was Jesus "made perfect" through his suffering? Does this imply he was somehow imperfect before? No. *Made perfect* really means brought to completion.

How could God fully identify and thus fully sympathize with us apart from becoming flesh and experiencing what our lives are like? The suffering of Jesus gave him that experience. It gave Jesus an unlimited capacity to sympathize with the troubles and temptations we experience in these bodies in this life.

No matter how much we suffer, we can never suffer beyond the ability of Jesus to sympathize with our suffering. We can never out-suffer Jesus. He knows and understands the hurts of living and dying in this world from his own personal, painful experience.

We can never out-suffer Jesus. He knows and understands the hurts of living and dying in this world from his own personal, painful experience.

He embraced the reality of our limitations (2:14)

Since the children have flesh and blood, he too shared in their humanity. (HEBREWS 2:14)

While you and I inherited the common trait of flesh and blood, Jesus chose it. He willingly took hold of something that didn't naturally belong to him so that he could enter the reality of our limitations.

You might think this simply means that Christ had a human body. But it is more than that. Verse 17 says, "For this reason he had to be made like his brothers in every way."

Jesus became absolutely human in body, mind, and emotions. He smelled like an infant, he thought like a child before he thought like a man, he felt the range of human emotions an adolescent feels, he experienced the realities of this world and the limitations of being human that we all experience—the limitations of time and space and flesh and blood. He got sleepy, his muscles ached after a hard day hammering nails in the carpenter's shop, his nose got sunburned, and his lips got chapped. And I wonder if his feelings got hurt and if he struggled to understand geometry.

He experienced the reality of our temptations (2:18)

Because he himself suffered when he was tempted, he is able to help those who are being tempted. (HEBREWS 2:18)

He is able to help us when we are tempted because he has been tempted too. We think it must have been easier for Jesus to resist the temptations Satan threw at him because, after all, he's God. But Jesus didn't exploit his inherent deity to overcome temptation. He faced it in his full humanity, using only the same weapons that we have at our disposal: the Word of God, the Holy Spirit, and trust in his heavenly Father.

When we feel tempted to do what is easy rather than what is right, Jesus knows how we feel. He was tempted that way too. When we feel overwhelmed with demands on our time and energy, Jesus knows how we feel. He knows what it is like for expectations to exceed physical and emotional energy.

When we feel crushed by the sorrows of this broken world, Jesus knows how we feel. Matthew writes that Jesus was overwhelmed with sorrow to the point of death (26:38).

Our Savior entered our reality, and he knows how it feels. We can go to God not only for salvation but also for sympathy.

When we feel overwhelmed with demands on our time and energy, Jesus knows how we feel. He knows what it is like for expectations to exceed physical and emotional energy.

Jesus Delivered Us from Slavery (2:14-15)

> *By his death he might destroy him who holds the power of death—that is, the devil—and free those who all their lives were held in slavery by their fear of death.* (HEBREWS 2:14-15)

The purpose of Jesus' life on earth was to deliver us from slavery. But to do that, he had to "destroy him who holds the power of death . . . the devil." How is it that Jesus' death destroyed the devil?

The only way for God to destroy Satan was to rob him of his weapon—death. Satan's weapon of death is extremely powerful. But if someone has a more powerful weapon than his or her enemy, the enemy's weapon becomes useless. And God has a weapon even more powerful than death—eternal life. With it, Jesus destroyed death. As John MacArthur wrote, "He went into death, through death, and came out on the other side, thereby conquering it."[6]

But when we read these verses, we find that we once again need to do a reality check. Because we know that the devil is obviously not destroyed yet.

Destroyed here means "rendered impotent," or "made powerless." The devil is far from destroyed in any final sense, but he no longer has the power to enslave us to sin or to the fear of sin's consequences—death. His power is limited. And one day, the devil will be destroyed completely.

A while ago, the trash man ran over my dog, Pepper. It didn't kill her; it just hurt her leg. And apparently, it made her very angry with all men who drive trucks and wear hats. So any big trucks driven by men with hats cannot exactly expect a welcome mat on our driveway. Many delivery people leave packages on the curb because of the terrifying way Pepper comes out to greet them.

But we have an electric fence. And the electric fence keeps Pepper in a defined area. The pain of electric shock is stronger than her will to go outside the fence. She might intimidate people outside that fence with her growling and barking, but she is limited. She can't go outside the fence.

Likewise, the devil is still active. He is vicious in his desire to destroy us. But he is limited by the superman of our salvation—Jesus—who has taken away from him his weapon of eternal death. While we still experience physical death, it is really only a passageway into eternity. We do not have to experience eternal spiritual death. And as our confidence in eternal life grows, physical death loses the power to enslave us to fear.

While we still experience physical death, it is really only a passageway into eternity. We do not have to experience eternal spiritual death. And as our confidence in eternal life grows, physical death loses the power to enslave us to fear.

Imagine being a slave who was set free but continued to live life as a slave. It doesn't make sense. We've been set free—so let's allow that freedom to change how we live. Let's allow it to change how we think about death. As we change how we think about death, it will change our feelings about death. We'll find that death won't seem so scary anymore. We'll be freed from slavery to the fear of death.

A person who has been freed from slavery to the fear of death can say with Paul, "To me, to live is Christ and to die is gain. . . . I desire to depart and be with Christ, which is better *by far*" (Philippians 1:21, 23, emphasis added).

Rather than our living with an inner terror about death, our hearts and minds can be at rest as we realize that death will one day release us into the presence of God. We can come to the place where the "something better" we desire is to depart and be with Christ—because we are confident it will not just be something better but something *far* better.

Jesus Paid Our Penalty (2:17)

> *He had to be made like his brothers in every way, . . . that he might make atonement for the sins of the people.* (HEBREWS 2:17)

Verse 14 says that Christ became like us so that he could die and render powerless the one who has the power of death—the devil. Verse 17 explains to us how Jesus takes away the devil's weapon—our sin that deserves death.[7]

Christ strips the devil of his power in death by making propitiation for our sins. That big word *propitiation* simply means Christ has done what is necessary to take away God's anger at us for our sins. God's justice is satisfied by Christ's sacrifice on the cross. Because Jesus has once and for all paid the debt for our sin and justice has been satisfied, the weapon of punishment by eternal death has been taken away from Satan.

Jesus Made Us His Family (2:11-12, 17)

> *Both the one who makes men holy and those who are made holy are of the same family. So Jesus is not ashamed to call them brothers.* (HEBREWS 2:11)

Here is good news for anyone who has been a slave to the fear of death: It doesn't matter who you are or what you've done. Through the death of Jesus, you can be a part of his family that will live forever.

He is not ashamed to call us his sisters and brothers. God is pleased with us, not because of who we are in ourselves or the earthly family we come from, but because of who we are in Christ.

When Jesus says he is our brother, he is saying, "We have the same Father, so I'm sharing my inheritance with you. I'm responsible for you; I am staying close to you; I will be loyal to you; I want to share life with you."

No one is part of God's family by birth. We become a part of his family by being reborn into it. Those in God's family share a trait more significant than red hair or blue eyes. We live free—free of controlling, defeating, anxiety-producing slavery to the fear of death. Can anyone see this family resemblance in you?

Jesus, our brother, has gone to the lengths of the cross so that we won't have to live in fear of death. But to live in this freedom, we have to listen to what he says and believe what he tells us in his Word. Let it speak to you and calm your fear.

Those in God's family share a trait more significant than red hair or blue eyes. We live free–free of controlling, defeating, anxiety-producing slavery to the fear of death.

Are you afraid of the unknowns beyond death's door? Jesus says, "Do not let your hearts be troubled. Trust in God; trust also in me. In my Father's house are many rooms; if it were not so, I would have told you. I am going there to prepare a place for you. And if I go and prepare a place for you, I will come back and take you to be with me that you also may be where I am" (John 14:1-3). It is not what you know but who you know that takes away the fear of the unknowns of death.

Do you fear the pain of losing someone or the pain your departure will leave behind? Jesus says, "I will ask the Father, and he will give you another Counselor to be with you forever—the Spirit of truth. The world cannot accept him, because it neither sees him nor knows him. But you know him, for he lives with you and will be in you. I will not leave you as orphans; I will come to you" (John 14:16-18). The promise of the presence of God in the person of the Holy Spirit and our confidence in the truth he speaks to us in the midst of our deep pain soothe our fear.

Do you fear the separation death brings from those you love? Paul said we should encourage one another with these words: "We do not want you to be uninformed, brothers, about those who are asleep, that you may not grieve as others do who have no hope. For since we believe that Jesus died and rose again, even so, through Jesus, God will bring with him those who have fallen asleep" (1 Thessalonians 4:13-14, ESV). Your separation will be short. You will be together again.

Do you fear the loss of control inherent in death? Peter invited us to follow Christ's example in trusting God with our lives and with our deaths. He wrote: "To this you were called, because Christ suffered for you, leaving you an example, that you should follow in his steps. . . . When he suffered, he made no threats. Instead, he entrusted himself to him who judges justly" (1 Peter 2:21, 23). The loss of control is real, but even more real is the trustworthiness of God.

Do you fear the finality of death? Paul encouraged us, "Do not lose heart. Though outwardly we are wasting away, yet inwardly we are being renewed day by day. For our light and momentary troubles are achieving for us an eternal glory that far outweighs them all. So we fix our eyes not on what is seen, but on what is unseen. For what is seen is temporary, but what is unseen is eternal" (2 Corinthians 4:16-18). Death is not the end for the believer. It is the beginning—the beginning of something better, something far better.

Do you fear facing the judgment that will follow death? Grab on to the truth from Romans 8, which says, "There is therefore now no condemnation for those who are in Christ Jesus. For the law of the Spirit of life has set you free in Christ Jesus from the law of sin and death" (verses 1-2, ESV). God will look at you and see you covered by his Son, and he will not judge you as your sins deserve.

We have to learn to tell ourselves the truth about life and death. And the source of truth is God's Word. When we listen to it and ingest it, it changes how we think and how we feel.

It has for me.

When Hope was a couple of weeks old, we went to the Christmas program at our church. As we sat in the balcony, enjoying the beauty of the music and pageantry, it hit me: I would never get to enjoy music with Hope. She would never sing in the children's choir. We would never sample rich desserts together, explore interesting places, or observe amazing art or architecture. Tears began to drip down my face and onto Hope as I began the process of letting go of the dreams I had for sharing with her all the good things life in this world has to offer.

But I also began to consider what was ahead for Hope. No, she wouldn't enjoy a fine orchestra here with me, but surely the music in the halls of heaven will be finer! As I thought through all the things I would not be able to share with her, I began to consider how much better heaven's version will be.

Over the coming weeks, I thought about other earthly things Hope would miss out on. She would miss out on allergies and acne, fighting weight gain and feeling left out, broken dreams and a broken heart. She would leave a world marked by crime and cruelty, disease and disappointment, for one of wholeness, richness, perfected beauty, and peace.

I began to see that Hope's brief life on this earth and quick deliverance into eternal life in the presence of God was not cruel or tragic. It was, in many ways, a gift to her, a protection from the evil to come. Not that it felt less cruel or tragic to me. I felt cheated. When Hope was about three months old, I wrote in my journal:

> I don't want to lose Hope. I would like to see her grow. I would like to know her as an adult. But I also know that this life is filled with pain. And I don't think it is a tragedy that she will have the opportunity to be spared from evil, from the pain of this life, and be in the presence of God. This is what I believe. It is not necessarily how I feel. But believing this is making a difference in how I feel.

I began to tell myself the truth about death and the reality of life in this world. And fear began to lose its grip on me.

I began to tell myself the truth about death and the reality of life in this world. And fear began to lose its grip on me.

Have you been a slave to the fear of death? Overprotective of your children? Haunted by the fear of losing your spouse or parents or best friend? Gripped by anxiety over a looming health issue?

It is okay to feel some fear over these things. But these fears do not have to consume you or enslave you. Jesus offers you something better.

Imagine living free from the fear of death. That is the very purpose for which Christ died. We can rest in the midst of the unknown, trusting God with our futures and recognizing that Jesus has removed the sting from death. As we walk in this freedom, we'll be able to give our lives away more freely, hold on to our loved ones more loosely, and embrace the adventure of life in Christ more fully.

Jesus has freed you from being a slave to fear.

You don't have to be scared to death of death.

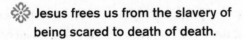

Jesus frees us from the slavery of being scared to death of death.

CHAPTER 3

where are you going?

HEBREWS 3:1–4:13

I AM MARRIED TO a frequent flier. Those of you who know a frequent flier know that I am not talking about how often my husband travels. It's about the points. *It is all about the points.* The nice part about being married to a frequent flier is that sometimes he shares his points with me!

Recently David got an e-mail explaining that his old points on his primary airline will be worth less after next year, so we figure it is time to do some cashing in. Besides, next year is our twentieth anniversary, so we've been trying to figure out where we want to go.

Of course for the vacation to be free (which is pretty much always our goal), we would have to be able to use points to get there and points for the hotel too.

David's company stays at one primary hotel chain, and he's been collecting some serious points with them. So last week we pulled out the book they publish with photographs of all their properties and began dreaming our way through it.

Obviously, they know what we want. In fact, in all the magazine and television advertising for vacation destinations, it is apparent that they know what we really want. . . .

We want romance—that's why the couples on the cruise line commercials and walking on the beach always look like they are so in love.

We want adventure—the people in these ads are not only beautiful people—they also have endless energy! They're climbing mountains and exploring ancient ruins and dancing until dawn.

We want to sleep as late as possible, in as much luxury as possible, and have somebody else make the bed!

But what I've noticed most about travel advertising is that we are always being sold relaxation. Look at the pictures. They all focus on the pool or the spa. They suck us in by inviting us to imagine ourselves lounging by that beautiful pool for the afternoon—or maybe even for the whole day.

But I'm starting to figure out something about vacations. Sometimes the planning for and dreaming about them are better than the reality of them. We dream and plan . . . and then we get there. We're married to the same unromantic guy and we have our same lethargic body and we're not about to put our cellulite on display at the pool for the day. Besides, the sun makes us sweat and the sand at the beach just gets in our clothes and . . . well, it just isn't what those ads and our imaginations made it out to be, is it?

And yet we keep searching. We keep looking for relief from the worries of the world, retreat from the problems that plague us, rest from the drudgery and work of our day-to-day lives.

We want to find a place where we can rest. Really rest.

MY SEARCH FOR REST

When my son, Matt, was born, I left my full-time job at a publishing company and started my own media relations business from home. From day one I was out to prove that I could work just as hard, be just as available, and accomplish just as much as I had before having a child. In those early years, not only was I having a hard time figuring out how to balance my new business with parenting, David and I were having a hard time figuring out how to share parenting, and I was having a hard time just with parenting itself. It didn't come very naturally or easily to me. I knew in my head it was important, but it didn't feel very important. It required more selflessness than I had anticipated. Whereas in my publicity job I was in control and knew what I was doing, in my mothering job I felt a total lack of control and little sense that I knew what I was doing.

The reality was that it had been such a long, long time since I had really talked to God, I didn't know where to start or if he would be willing to hear me.

A couple of years into it, I found myself on the brink of a crisis. Everything in my body seemed to be out of whack. In fact, one day David asked me, "Are you trying to see every medical specialist there is in a six-month period of time?" And it seemed like I was. I had been to the dermatologist and the pulmonologist and the gastroenterologist and the proctologist and the gynecologist and the urologist and the psychologist . . . and I wasn't getting any better.

About that time we were making a move to Nashville. Before we even moved, I began the search for a doctor in Nashville who would help me figure out what was going on with my body.

But I also felt deep inside that these were not just physical issues. I knew that in addition to physical and emotional burnout, I was on empty spiritually. Not that I wasn't busy for God. But the busyness was empty. David and I were involved in our church, and I was doing publicity for Christian authors. But I had a tremendous fear. My greatest fear was that someone would ask me the question, "What is God doing in your life right now?"

Oh, I would have found a way to answer it to make myself look good by talking about a ministry I was involved in or a book I was working on or an issue or idea that made me appear spiritually aware.

But the truth was, I wasn't allowing God to be at work in me or on me or through me. Because while I was busy in my church and traveling in Christian circles, I wasn't talking to him or listening to him by reading his Word. The reality was that it had been such a long, long time since I had really talked to God, I didn't know where to start or if he would be willing to hear me.

Somehow moving across the country gave me the opportunity to make a fresh start. I had always thought Bible studies were nice for people who did them—people who had the time for them—but honestly, I didn't think I needed one. After all, I had grown up in church and minored in Bible in college, so I thought I pretty much knew the Bible.

But I was desperate to hear God speak into my falling-apart-at-the-seams life, so I visited a weekly intensive Bible study soon after we arrived in Nashville. I remember that first week the lecturer was talking about the woman in the Gospels who had been hemorrhaging blood for twelve years. The speaker said, "The life was literally draining out of her." I thought, "That's me! I feel like the life is draining out of me." She talked about how the woman reached out to touch Jesus, telling him that she needed a miracle. The lecturer asked if anyone there needed a miracle. I wanted to raise my hand or stand up and wave.

I knew I needed nothing less than a miracle to break through the years of stony silence between God and me, the pileup of unconfessed sin, the layers of indifference, the well-rehearsed facade of spirituality I had perfected.

I was tired of it. I wanted something real. I wanted it badly enough that I was willing to make a commitment to the weekly study with its daily questions, which seemed like a huge sacrifice at the time. For me, making that commitment was my way of saying to God, "Knowing you is more important than being available to my clients on Wednesday mornings, more important than maintaining my 'I already know it all' image, more important than just about anything else."

I was tired of feeling like a hypocrite.

> The rest God offers is deep, lasting, all-encompassing rest—not just for our bodies, but for our souls.

Can you relate? Do you find yourself feeling like a hypocrite at times—going through all the motions of religion and yet finding that there is a void, a sense of deadness toward and distance from God? Have you settled for something less than a genuine love relationship with Jesus? Do you want something better—a relationship that is real, a faith that is relevant?

Or perhaps you can't relate to that. Hypocrisy is not your problem because you've never even considered yourself a religious person. You've seen religion as something for other people, and you're not at all interested in becoming religious for religion's sake. Perhaps it is the hypocrisy you think you see in others that bothers you, and you've rejected faith altogether because you certainly don't want to become one of "them." But to know God in a powerful way, a way that is real—that appeals to you.

God does not intend for us to wear ourselves out with meaningless religious activity, filling ourselves with theology, working for him but never knowing what it is to enjoy knowing him and being known by him. Neither does he intend for us to go through this life on our own, unaware of him or estranged from him.

There is something better. And it is not working harder or trying harder. It doesn't require more sacrifice on our part. All it requires is that we receive what he wants to give to us—that we enter into what he has prepared for us.

God is offering us something better . . . and that something better is rest. Real rest. Rest from the weariness of feeling that we can never measure up to God's standards, rest from trying to be good enough or do enough to earn God's favor. The something better is resting in what Christ has done for us, resting in knowing him and being known by him.

God is holding out to you the gift of rest, the kind of rest that only he can provide.

In Hebrews 3 and 4, the writer is letting us know that real rest is within our grasp. It is more than just a glossy picture on a page. Real rest is not just a mirage that doesn't deliver. The rest God offers is deep, lasting, all-encompassing rest—not just for our bodies, but for our souls.

In the introduction to this book, we noted the numerous times the writer of Hebrews says, "Let us . . ." as an encouragement in moving forward with God. Hebrews 4 has the first one we've come to so far in our study, found in 4:11. "Let us, therefore, make every effort to enter that rest." It almost sounds like a contradiction, doesn't it? Make every effort . . . to rest?

But the writer to the Hebrews knows about us. He knows that rest is what we want and need. But he also knows we can be very aimless in our pursuit of it. We can expend a lot of effort and energy thinking we're moving in that direction, only to find we're running in place or just going in circles.

Where are you going? Are you moving forward toward rest? If not, what is keeping you from it?

WHAT KEEPS US FROM REAL REST?

In chapter 3 of Hebrews, we see several snapshots of God's people in search of rest. That was the promise of the Promised Land of Canaan—a place where the Israelites would no longer be slaves of Pharaoh. They would finally be at home. They could finally put down roots and really rest. And yet, as surely as the Promised Land was theirs for the taking and as much as they wanted it, something kept them from entering the rest that God held out to them. The writer to the Hebrews wants us to see what kept them from rest so we can avoid the same aimless wandering in the desert and ultimately dying in the wilderness that those children of Israel experienced. So he spells out exactly what caused them to die in the desert rather than enter the rest of the Promised Land.

Hardness of Heart (3:7-11)

> *So, as the Holy Spirit says: "Today, if you hear his voice, do not harden your hearts as you did in the rebellion, during the time of testing in the desert, where your fathers tested and tried me and for forty years saw what I did."* (HEBREWS 3:7-9)

What does hardness of heart look like, and how can we diagnose it?

We know what it looked like in the children of Israel when they were in the desert. Things weren't going exactly the way they wanted, so they grumbled and complained and quarreled and disobeyed. These were the outward manifestations of an internal problem—hardness of heart.

And there were consequences. No one who was over the age of twenty at the time of the Exodus entered the Promised Land, except Joshua and Caleb. The others were buried in the desert. Rest was waiting, but they couldn't enter into it because they had allowed their hearts to harden.

So what makes hearts hard, and how can we keep ours from becoming hardened?

Sometimes broken hearts become hard hearts. Have you ever broken something and then glued it back together? Sometimes when we do that it becomes so solid and stiff that nothing could ever break it again. When our hearts are broken, they either become softer and more pliable, or they become hardened. The broken places in our lives can become the places where we fall into the arms of God and accept his offer of rest, or they can make us stiff and resistant to God, resentful toward God.

Don't let your hurts harden you against God. Let your hurts become the places where God can work on you to mold you into his likeness as you stay soft toward him.

Hardness of heart is also something we develop when we experience conviction of sin but we choose not to repent.

A while ago I bought a new pair of shoes for walking in the park near my house. I noticed right away that they were rubbing a place on the side of my heel, but I ignored it because . . . well, because I'm cheap and I didn't want to buy another new pair since I was past being able to return these. So I kept wearing them, and for a couple of months they made that place on the side of my heel red and sore when I wore them.

But after a while, that place wasn't sore anymore when I wore the shoes. They still rubbed that spot, but I had developed a callous. In fact, I haven't worn those shoes for almost six months now and I still have the callous. After the callous developed, I didn't feel the rubbing so much anymore. A hardness had developed, so I hardly noticed the rub.

The broken places in our lives can become the places where we fall into the arms of God and accept his offer of rest, or they can make us stiff and resistant to God, resentful toward God.

The same thing can happen to our hearts. God speaks to us through a sermon we hear, a passage of Scripture we read, or something a friend shares with us, and our hearts are pricked. Maybe they get pricked and pricked. Sometimes our hearts have been pricked so many times and we've ignored it so long that we don't even feel the prick anymore. We've built up a callous to conviction. Our hearts have become hard.

Have you felt a prick in your conscience about how much money you're spending on yourself while giving so little to God and to those in need? Have you felt the prick of conviction about choosing sleep over time alone with God? Have you felt the nudge to forgive?

Have you found yourself ignoring the prompting of the Holy Spirit, hoping that feeling of conviction will just go away? It will with time. If you keep ignoring it, your heart will become hard and you won't feel that prick anymore. And when you realize that has happened, it will be the saddest day of your life.

Don't let your heart become hard by ignoring the conviction of sin in your life.

Believing a Lie (3:12-15)

Encourage one another daily, as long as it is called Today, so that none of you may be hardened by sin's deceitfulness. (HEBREWS 3:13)

Sin begins when we believe a lie. We put others down because we believe the lie that if they are diminished, we will be respected. We spend exorbitant amounts of money on ourselves because we believe the lie that a better wardrobe and a more beautiful house will make us happier. We invite people into our homes via television programs, believing the lie that it is just entertainment, that we're mature enough to not be affected by it, and that most of the double entendre will just go over our kids' heads.

When we believe these lies rather than confronting them with the truth, we allow the world to shape our perspectives. Then we find that we can hardly tell the truth from the lies.

Only by saturating our minds with Scripture can we be equipped to recognize the voice of the liar in our lives and avoid the deceitfulness of sin that will rob us of rest.

Only by saturating our minds with Scripture can we be equipped to recognize the voice of the liar in our lives and avoid the deceitfulness of sin that will rob us of rest.

Disobedience from Unbelief (3:16-19)

To whom did God swear that they would never enter his rest if not to those who disobeyed? So we see that they were not able to enter, because of their unbelief. (HEBREWS 3:18-19)

When we see the word *unbelief,* most of us quickly think to ourselves, "That's not me. I believe!" But do we? Really?

The children of Israel would have said they believed in God, and yet they didn't believe God's promise that he would give them victory over the giants in the land. Therefore they didn't obey God to go in and take the land.

Is there a giant in the landscape of your life that has you intimidated? What unbelief is keeping you out of the land of God's blessing because you don't believe God is big enough or powerful enough or good enough to help you overcome it?

What has God called you to do and promised to equip you for, but you haven't entered into because you don't really believe he will equip you for it?

What sin keeps you bound by shame even though God has told you that he has forgiven you, because you don't really believe he has forgiven you?

How many nights are you going to cry yourself to sleep, refusing to call out to God in your loneliness, because you don't really believe he can or will fill your emptiness?

What has God told you about himself clearly in his Word that you simply do not believe? How long will you let unbelief keep you from real rest?

Disobedience is the choice we make when we choose not to believe. We don't follow God's instructions to move forward in doing what he wants us to do. We try to kill our sense of shame by doing shameful things. We do desperate things in an effort to assuage our loneliness. These are acts of disobedience that flow from unbelief.

What unbelief has led to disobedience in your life? Won't you choose to believe God's Word and thereby enter the rest of God?

ENTERING INTO REAL REST

Long after the Hebrew people entered the Promised Land of Canaan, God is still holding out to his people an offer of rest. It's not too late to get in on it. Let's look together at Hebrews 4 to find out how we can enter into the rest that God gives.

> *The promise of entering his rest still stands.* (Hebrews 4:1)

What is this rest that God is offering to give to us?

First and foremost, it is the rest of salvation. To enter God's rest is to be at peace with God, free from guilt and from feelings of guilt. To enter God's rest means that the aimless search for the source of truth is over. We've found truth in the person of Jesus. Entering God's rest means we surrender our "self-effort" salvation. It is the end of trying to please God with our own feeble, fleshly works. It is resting in the grace and provision of God.[8]

Repentance is the first step toward rest. We take a step toward God and away from our own sinfulness as well as our self-righteousness, and in love he meets us there. With each step toward him, we enter more deeply into his rest.

To enter God's rest means that we no longer have to depend on ourselves or our own resources. We can lean on God, confident that he will never fail us. We can depend on him for everything we need, in every situation.

God's rest is for right now, as we choose to trust him. He invites us to walk away from fearfulness and worry and anxiety and enter into the rest that is only found in him.

Rest is another name for *life*—life as God meant it to be.

Falling Short of Real Rest

While Hebrews 4:1 has an invitation, it also has a warning.

> *Since the promise of entering his rest still stands, let us be careful that none of you be found to have fallen short of it.* (HEBREWS 4:1)

Tad Porter is a friend of ours who is an amazing oncologist. If I get cancer, I'm going to see Tad. But sometimes his brain works faster than his tongue. A while ago he was praying during our Sunday night small group, and he said, "Lord, forgive our falling shorts." The giggles kind of put a stop to our serious prayer time.

The kind of "falling short" this passage is talking about is not about our pants falling down, nor is it about our personal moral failures, the mistakes we make. This is the ultimate falling short, the ultimate failure to grab hold of Christ and enter his rest.

In the New Living Translation this verse reads, "We ought to tremble with fear that some of you might fail to experience it." Here we learn that there is something worth being afraid of—terrified of—in this life: unbelief, not trusting God. It is a scary thing to hear and know the promises of God and to choose not to trust them—to decide we don't really need them or want them, to walk away from them rather than enter into them.

Now we might read this verse and think that the writer is suggesting that we should be afraid all the time that we might fall short. And we might think he means that we are supposed to live our lives fearing we will miss heaven because of the many ways we fall short of living what we believe. But this is not what he is suggesting. As we rest in the promises of God, we can be fearless as we live our lives in this threatening world. We can face death and face God without fear. We don't have to live with constant uneasiness.

We feel uneasy only when we are tempted not to trust God's promises. And that uneasiness sends us running back into the arms of God, back into the safe place of assurance and rest.

Choosing to Trust

> *We also have had the gospel preached to us, just as they did; but the message they heard was of no value to them, because those who heard did not combine it with faith.* (HEBREWS 4:2)

Who is the "they" and "them" the writer is talking about? He's talking about the children of Israel out in the desert. Israel had heard the "gospel" preached (that is, the good news brought by Caleb and Joshua that the land was theirs for the taking). But their response to that good news was lacking. Even though they had seen the Red Sea part and the pillars of cloud and fire, even though they had eaten manna every day, now as they were faced with a new challenge they simply didn't trust God. And they didn't enter the rest of the Promised Land God was holding out to them.

What kind of faith is necessary to have real rest in this life? Faith that trusts God wholeheartedly with our lives, faith that leaves behind the desert existence of expecting this world to meet our needs, faith that moves forward with God into the life he is holding out to us.

Verse 3 says, "We who have believed enter that rest." So those who wholeheartedly trust enter that rest. Here we see that the faith that pleases God is more than just a mental acceptance that something is true. It is a belief that blossoms into trust. Deeply trusting God with our lives is what gives rest to our souls.

Combining active trust with simple belief leads to real rest. It does no good to hear the gospel if we don't go to Christ for salvation, if we don't believe it, if we don't respond to it in faith.

We trust that his sacrifice on the cross was enough to satisfy the justice of God on our behalf, and we rest in the salvation Jesus provides. We trust that because of his character, we can depend on him to do what is right with us and with this world. We trust that he will make good on all his promises to us, so we can rest. The more we trust him, the deeper our rest.

It is a sad reality that many people will not enter God's ultimate rest in eternity because they never moved from knowing about God and knowing about the Bible and going to church to knowing God personally, trusting him completely, joining themselves wholly to him through faith.

The other sad reality is that there are many Christians who never enjoy the rest God holds out to them even in this life because while they chose to trust him once for salvation, they stopped there. The Christian life is not simply about that one time you trusted God for salvation. It is a day-by-day, hour-by-hour, ongoing trust in the promises of God to save you, sustain you, and satisfy you.

The Christian life is not simply about that one time you trusted God for salvation. It is a day-by-day, hour-by-hour, ongoing trust in the promises of God to save you, sustain you, and satisfy you.

Are you ready for something better than living with a constant sense of uneasiness and unrest? Would you choose to trust God with your eternal salvation? Not only that, would you trust him with your children, with your marriage, with your health crisis, with your financial situation, with your future? Will you choose to trust God and enter into the rest he has for you?

Embrace the promise of verse 3: "We who have believed enter that rest."

No More Working Your Way to God (4:10-11)

> *Anyone who enters God's rest also rests from his own work, just as God did from his.* (HEBREWS 4:10)

I grew up working in my dad's drugstore. As soon as I could reach the cash register, I was working at the front counter for ten cents an hour. And I've always worked since then. I worked in an office supply store and a china and card shop. I worked during my college years, and two weeks after I graduated from college I got a job at a publishing company. Then, a few weeks after I gave birth to my son, Matt, I started my own media relations business.

I've always enjoyed earning my own money and paying my own way. I hate to owe somebody money. I'd much rather have someone else owe me money than be in that person's debt.

And I suppose this carries over into my relationship with God. I want to pay my dues. I want to earn my way in and earn my keep. But that's not how it works with God. And the truth is, I don't have anything of value to offer God to buy my way in.

I want to pay my dues. I want to earn my way in and earn my keep. But that's not how it works with God. And the truth is, I don't have anything of value to offer God to buy my way in.

Jesus said, "Blessed are the poor in spirit" (Matthew 5:3). He was saying that to come to God in faith is to come empty handed, with nothing to offer—no capital, no resources, no special abilities. It is to open our hands and our hearts to receive. That is the humble act of wholehearted trusting that is required of us.

Aren't you tired of working hard to earn God's favor? Would you accept that you can never pay for or earn your way into his family? Would you believe that salvation is the gift of God—a gift, pure and simple, that you can't work to earn? And would you be content in that and enjoy that and unwrap the gift of real rest that he has given you?

Opening Up under God's Word (4:12-13)

> *The word of God is living and active. Sharper than any double-edged sword, it penetrates even to dividing soul and spirit, joints and marrow; it judges the thoughts and attitudes of the heart. Nothing in all creation is hidden from God's sight. Everything is uncovered and laid bare before the eyes of him to whom we must give account.* (HEBREWS 4:12-13)

Here, I think, is perhaps the most important key for living in the here-and-now, daily resting in Christ.

The Word of God is living enough–active enough–to penetrate us and change us. Then we don't have to live with an overwhelming sense of hypocrisy, so that the faith we claim can become an increasing reality in the way we live.

A lot of people like the Bible. They like to pick parts of it that appeal to them. And they conveniently ignore or explain away the parts they don't like or don't understand. We're all prone to doing that.

Hebrews 4:12-13 tells us that if we really want to experience rest, instead of placing ourselves in authority over Scripture, we need to open up our lives under its authority. We make ourselves accountable to its expectations, submit ourselves to its demands, accept its truth. Rather than judging its validity, we allow the Word of God to judge our thoughts and motives.

The Word of God is living enough—active enough—to penetrate us and change us. When it does, we don't have to live with an overwhelming sense of hypocrisy, so that the faith we claim can become an increasing reality in the way we live.

In our first house we had some unwelcome guests—mice and roaches. I'll never forget one time when David was traveling. In the middle of the night, the trap behind the washing machine caught a mouse. The bad news was, it didn't kill him. For hours he flapped around behind the washer, banging it with the trap, completely freaking me out!

Now the mice were bad, but the roaches were even worse. I would flip on the light in the kitchen and roaches would scamper across the counter and in and out of the stovetop. Pretty picture, isn't it?

In a way, this is a picture of what the Word of God does. It throws on a light in the dark places of our lives and reveals the sin that has made itself at home. It shows us what we need to see about ourselves so we can root it out and kill it off.

Let me give you another mental picture: You will never enter deep rest until you come to grips with the experience of spiritual nakedness. Rest requires that we come clean with God, get it all out in the open.

I used to tape the television show *Extreme Makeover* and then fast-forward to the end just to see the before and after pictures. Isn't it fun to see what thousands of dollars of plastic surgery can do?

Did you know that God has chosen us for "extreme makeovers"? Most of us come to the Word of God looking for advice to help us fix ourselves up a little, only to discover that God wants to do something far more dramatic and intense.

This makeover is a lifelong process, and the tool God uses is his Word, which cuts deeply and lays bare the ugliness we might wish to keep hidden. He cuts away what is keeping us from displaying the beauty of his presence in our lives. And the cutting away can be painful—initially.

It always surprises me that the people on these makeover shows are willing to have their photographs taken wearing only their underwear for the whole world to see. I would never want to be that exposed! And neither do I relish the idea of having my inner life exposed, my thought life and motives laid bare. But I am unable to hide anything from God's penetrating gaze. And I don't have to be afraid.

As he exposes my shallow beliefs and false intentions with the truth of his Word, he is able to cut away what displeases him, and I am better for the exposure. Until he cuts it away, I can never fully rest.

As he exposes my shallow beliefs and false intentions with the truth of his Word, he is able to cut away what displeases him, and I am better for the exposure. Until he cuts it away, I can never fully rest.

Are you willing to open yourself up to the whole Word of God for an extreme makeover? Would you allow the Great Physician to cut deep?

He will transform your inner ugliness so that you radiate his glory, and he will clothe you with his own righteousness so that you display his holiness. He will cut away what is keeping you from real rest.

FINALLY . . . REST

It was a year or so after I started the in-depth study of the Bible when one morning at church I was looking over the songs we would be singing in the worship service. Ever the critic, I expressed my disappointment to David that we were going to sing a song that is on my unofficial "I can go my whole life without ever singing that song again" list. It was the chorus "Peace Like a River." I suppose I had sung it so many times in youth group growing up that it just seemed like a silly chorus designed to fill time.

And then it came time to sing, and I began, "I've got peace like a river, I've got peace like a river, I've got peace like a river in my soul. . . . I've got joy like a fountain, I've got joy like a fountain. . . . I've got love for my Jesus, I've got love for my Jesus. . . ."

Except I could barely sing. Because as I began to sing, I realized it was true! So deeply true, I began to weep. I realized I wasn't going through the motions anymore. The words were now filled with meaning. God was at work in my life, and something real was happening. I was changing. I had real peace and real joy, and I didn't feel like a hypocrite anymore.

I had found the "something better" I'd been looking for. I had found rest. Rest in trusting God with not only my eternal salvation but with my day-to-day problems and challenges. I'd found rest from all my work of trying to please God without the power that comes from being connected to him. I'd found rest in opening up my life under the scrutiny of God's Word and letting him clean out what is displeasing to him.

TODAY IS THE DAY

Aren't you tired? Tired of trying so hard to please God on your own?

Won't you combine your belief in God with faith and rest in God's provision for you in Jesus? Will you enter into the rest God is holding out to you?

Would you choose to unite your understanding of the gospel with a decision to trust Jesus with your life and find the rest you have always longed for?

Today, if you hear his voice, do not harden your hearts. (HEBREWS 4:7)

Anyone who hears God's voice and God's promises and chooses to place her faith in them, trusting God to bring her to the place of rest he has prepared for those who love him, will enter that rest.

Can you hear the voice of Jesus saying to you, "Come to me, all you who are weary and burdened, and I will give you rest" (Matthew 11:28)?

"Today, if you hear his voice . . ." Today is the day to start that journey if you've not yet begun. Don't put it off. Don't allow your heart to become hardened. Don't allow unbelief to take you in the wrong direction. Don't let disobedience rob you of real joy. Don't be deceived by sin and trapped by its damning power.

Hebrews 4:1 says that the promise of rest still stands. It is not too late for your rebellious child or your unbelieving husband. It is not too late for your skeptical sibling or your cynical friend. It is not too late for you. God's rest is still open. No one is ever too far gone for God to draw him or her into his rest.

But the opportunity to enter God's rest will not remain open indefinitely. Today, right now, is the only day, the only opportunity we can be sure of.

One of the frustrating things about trying to use frequent-flier miles is that we often find out we've waited too long to make use of them. There are no more seats available on the flights we need, no more rooms available at the hotel we want. So if we want to go somewhere, we have to be diligent. We have to plan ahead, knowing where we want to go and how we intend to get there.

Hebrews 4:11 says, "Let us, therefore, make every effort to enter that rest." God has opened to you the rest that he himself enjoys. Are you making every effort to enter that rest?

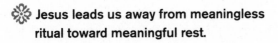

Jesus leads us away from meaningless ritual toward meaningful rest.

CHAPTER 4

what do you need?

HEBREWS 4:14–5:10; 7:1-28

I LIVE IN NASHVILLE. And in Nashville, we see ourselves as very cool and connected. We see big stars at the grocery store and act like it's no big deal. We've got connections. We know people on the inside. And we love it.

Recently Matt's basketball coach was on *The Tonight Show* and then took a red-eye flight home after the taping to be back in time to coach Matt's game the next afternoon. I'd tell you who it is, but then I'd hate to be a name-dropper.

I pity the poor people who work for the artist-management companies and record labels in this city. Because when there's a great concert, I'm sure they're deluged with calls. They suddenly discover they have 5 million best friends who all want backstage passes.

Have you ever had a backstage pass? Those are cool. When you have one, you can flash it to the guy on guard and walk right through the curtain into the greenroom. You can meet the artist. You don't have to try to talk your way in or be timid. You're cleared in advance. You've been granted all access.

God wants to draw you close—for your life to be a day-by-day experience of being close to him, connected to him. Drawing near to God is the essence of Christianity.

But this is just a dream for most of us. We're much more familiar with what it feels like to be locked out, left out. We know what it is to have no connections. To be a nobody—wanting in, but not welcome.

Some of us have felt that way when it comes to God. We're not sure if we've got what it takes. We didn't grow up in church, or we've been gone for so long it seems foreign to us. We don't feel like we fit in. We don't know the lingo. We're interested in getting to know God, but we know we're not good enough to get in on our own.

The writer to the Hebrews recognizes that access to God is not just something we desire; it's what we need. He knows we need to draw near to God. We see it several times in Hebrews, including in these verses:

> *Let us draw near with confidence to the throne of grace.* (Hebrews 4:16, NASB)

> *A better hope is introduced, by which we draw near to God.* (Hebrews 7:19)

> *He is able also to save forever those who draw near to God through Him.* (Hebrews 7:25, NASB)

God wants to draw you close—for your life to be a day-by-day experience of being close to him, connected to him. Drawing near to God is the essence of Christianity.

WHAT WILL IT TAKE TO GAIN ACCESS?

But how can we do it? How can we gain access? Who do we know who can get us in? We need a connection, a mediator—someone who will make our case and gain access for us. We need someone with the clout and the confidence and the compassion to get us in. While we may never have defined it this way before, what we need is a priest.

A priest is a go-between, someone to represent us before God. We're sinful, and we can't approach God directly. We need someone who can—someone who is holy and acceptable to enter God's presence on our behalf, someone who is authorized and appointed and equipped for this role—a priest—to bring us to God.

When the writer to the Hebrews wrote to the believers in the little house church in Rome,* they didn't need to be convinced that they needed a priest. Their whole religious lives had revolved around the Temple system of priests offering sacrifices on their behalf.

In fact, the priesthood was a center point of Judaism. No sacrifices could be made except by the priest, and no forgiveness could be found apart from the sacrifices. Some Jewish Christians had begun to feel insecure about leaving this familiar system. They wanted to embrace Jesus but hold on to the sacrificial system, too.

Even as he explains the weaknesses of the old Levitical priest system, the writer of Hebrews is not trying to convince his readers that it was a bad thing—just that it was incomplete and temporary. It was never intended to be permanent. From its inception, it was meant to be a picture, an illustration that would prepare people for the perfect priest to come. God ordained this system to show us our need for cleansing from sin, our need for someone to be a mediator between us and God.

The writer to the Hebrews was telling them that now that a greater priest had come who could meet all their needs forever, they could let go of their attachment to the old priestly system. They now needed to grab on to the superior, perfect, permanent priest provided by God in his Son, Jesus Christ.

But it is hard to let go of what we've depended on in the past, isn't it? It is hard to let go of what has brought us a sense of security. We tend to like what is familiar.

Today we have our own ways of making ourselves acceptable to God—ways we've become comfortable with. We depend on being good people, we depend

*Various commentators suggest differing locations for the recipients of the letter to the Hebrews. John MacArthur writes that perhaps they were somewhere near Greece (John MacArthur, *The MacArthur New Testament Commentary: Hebrews* [Chicago, Moody Press, 1983], x). R. Kent Hughes writes that because the author conveys greetings of several Italian Christians who were with him (13:24), perhaps the letter was written to Jewish Christians on Italian soil, likely in or around Rome (R. Kent Hughes, *Hebrews: An Anchor for the Soul* [Wheaton, IL: Crossway Books], 1:18). Raymond Brown writes in *The Message of Hebrews* (Downers Grove, IL: InterVarsity Press, 1982, 17), "As to the precise location of this group or church we cannot be sure. Some have suggested Jerusalem, and other places in Palestine have also been named. Alexandria has also been considered as a possible destination, but Rome is the most likely location."

on working hard in the church, and we depend on being from a religious family. We struggle to put our faith completely in a more perfect mediator, a more perfect advocate.

So we, too, need to see that Jesus is the ultimate, perfect, superior intermediary to plead our case before God. He will make us acceptable to God, provide access to God, and give us entry into his presence so that we can draw near.

THE PRIEST WE'VE ALWAYS NEEDED

In chapters 4 and 5 of Hebrews, the writer shows us what an ideal human priest is like and draws some obvious comparisons to the perfect priest, Jesus. (He takes a little sidebar in 5:11–6:20, which we'll look at in the next chapter.) In chapter 7, he moves from comparing Jesus' priesthood to the Levitical priests descended from Aaron, to comparing Jesus to the mysterious priest Melchizedek, who lived some five hundred years before the priesthood was established through Aaron.

All of this is to make clear to us that Jesus is the perfect priest. He's everything we could want or need in a mediator.

Isn't it a relief to know that the one who represents us before God understands what it is like to live in this world?

He Understands (4:15)

> *Since we have a great high priest who has gone through the heavens, Jesus the Son of God, let us hold firmly to the faith we profess. For we do not have a high priest who is unable to sympathize with our weaknesses, but we have one who has been tempted in every way, just as we are—yet was without sin.* (Hebrews 4:14-15)

We're naturally skeptical of anyone who offers advice or assistance if they've never been where we are. What alcoholic wants to take advice on how to handle walking past a liquor store from someone who has never had a drink? Who wants to trust a nurse who says, "It won't hurt a bit," if she has never had a shot?

Isn't it a relief to know that the one who represents us before God understands what it is like to live in this world?

Jesus was tempted in all the ways we are. Jesus was tempted to lie to make himself look good. Jesus was tempted to cut corners in the carpenter's shop to make a few extra bucks. Jesus was tempted to take a long, lustful look at a pretty girl when she walked by. Jesus was tempted to dishonor his parents when they seemed simpleminded. Jesus was tempted to covet someone else's home when he had no home of his own. Jesus was tempted to seek revenge when someone he loved was senselessly murdered.

Jesus doesn't roll his eyes and wonder how we could even consider taking a step in the direction we're being tempted in. He doesn't take lightly our struggles with sin, because he knows what it is like to be tempted. Jesus was tempted in all the ways we are—yet he never gave in to sin.

Jesus doesn't roll his eyes and wonder how we could even consider taking a step in the direction we're being tempted in. He doesn't take lightly our struggles with sin, because he knows what it is like to be tempted.

We might think that if Jesus never sinned, he really doesn't know what temptation is like. But if you think about it, only the person who tries to resist temptation knows how strong it is. The one who gives in after a few minutes doesn't know what it would be like after a few hours. Who has experienced greater temptation: the one who is tempted and quickly gives in to the temptation or the one who holds on and holds out and doesn't give in? Christ, in never yielding to temptation, knows more about the strength of temptation and the suffering involved in temptation than we will ever know.[9] He's our advocate who understands.

He's Approachable (4:14-16)

I told you earlier that my husband, David, is Mr. Frequent Flier. Occasionally when he cashes in points we get to fly first class, which is really fun. When you're in first class and they pull the curtain closed between cabins, you can't help but have a sense of superiority over the riffraff in the back.

But most often *I am* the riffraff in the back.

First class is nice when you're up front, but there's something annoying about it when you're not—especially when the flight attendant snaps the curtain in place to create a barrier between the privileged few in first class and us peons in coach. That curtain snapping shut just seems to rub it in, doesn't it? Have you ever tried to use the restroom in first class when you're seated in coach, and some snooty flight attendant tells you to head to the back of the plane?

In the old priestly system, people knew a lot about a curtain that kept them out. God had made his home in the Holy of Holies in the Temple. But people were not welcome to enter; they were locked out of God's presence. Once a year one person—the high priest—entered the Most Holy Place on the Day of Atonement. And just in case he died while he was in there, the others tied a rope to his leg so they could pull him out, because no one else could go in.

> We receive mercy for our past failures and grace to meet our present and future needs. He gives us the mercy and grace we need in his perfect timing—just when we need it.

For centuries, the Jewish people knew what it was to be unable to approach God. But the hour that Jesus died, Matthew records, "When Jesus had cried out again in a loud voice, he gave up his spirit. At that moment the curtain of the temple was torn in two from top to bottom" (Matthew 27:50-51). From that moment on, there was no longer a barrier between God and his people.

The writer to the Hebrews wants us to make the most of this opportunity. "Let us then approach the throne of grace with confidence, so that we may receive mercy and find grace to help us in our time of need" (4:16).

Let us approach really means "let us constantly approach." This is not a one-time thing. It is a daily, hourly, minute-by-minute opportunity. The sacrifice of Jesus made a way for us to enter the presence of God continually. It also supplies what we need to enter the presence of God confidently. We can draw near to God knowing we're wanted and welcome, not cowering in shame or wondering if we'll be rejected.

Notice that this is not a throne of judgment. This is a throne of grace—the epitome of grace. The ruler on this throne doesn't deal in intimidation; he gives grace. We don't have to be afraid or ashamed. We can draw near with confidence that we will be accepted and wanted and provided for.

We will "receive mercy and find grace to help us in our time of need" (Hebrews 4:16). We receive mercy for our past failures and grace to meet our present and future needs. He gives us the mercy and grace we need in his perfect timing—just when we need it.

Do you need it right now, today? Wouldn't it be a shame to waste one more year, one more month, one more day on the fringes of real relationship with God because you've believed the lie that you are not good enough or not welcome enough to boldly approach God for the mercy and grace you need?

He's Our Perfect Sacrifice (5:1-6)

> *Every high priest is selected from among men and is appointed to represent them in matters related to God, to offer gifts and sacrifices for sins. . . . No one takes this honor upon himself; he must be called by God, just as Aaron was.*
> (HEBREWS 5:1, 4)

A man could not become a priest just because he aspired to it. This was not a career choice but a divine calling. And the most critical part of the job description for a high priest was to make sacrifices for the people's sins.

Think for a minute about what it meant as a priest to spend every day slaughtering animals for sacrifices.

And while the sacrifices of animals covered sin, they didn't take away the tendency or capacity to sin. The whole process and ritual was calculated to keep people at a distance from God rather than bring them near.

> *He has to offer sacrifices for his own sins, as well as for the sins of the people.*
> (HEBREWS 5:3)

Even the finest of Levitical priests had to offer sacrifices for their own sin. But Jesus had no sin. And that made him not only the perfect priest but also the perfect sacrifice.

Hebrews 7:27 shows us how Jesus is superior as both a priest and as a sacrifice: "Unlike the other high priests, he does not need to offer sacrifices day after day, first for his own sins, and then for the sins of the people. He sacrificed for their sins once for all when he offered himself."

In fact, all the sacrifices that the high priest offered pointed to Jesus. The

> In one perfect sacrifice, Jesus accomplished what thousands of blood-drenched animal sacrifices made by a multitude of priests never accomplished.

years upon years of offering animal sacrifices to cover sin pointed to one thing—the need for a perfect sacrifice. And in one perfect sacrifice, Jesus accomplished what thousands of blood-drenched animal sacrifices made by a multitude of priests never accomplished. He opened the way to God permanently, so that anyone at any time can enter into the presence of God through Jesus.

Jesus' sacrifice was once and for all. It did not have to be repeated. And rather than providing momentary, partial forgiveness, his sacrifice provided pervasive, eternal forgiveness.

Do you know what this means for you? God is not waiting for you to figure out how you are going to make things right, how you are going to even the scales for the wrongs you have done. In one sacrifice, because of its supreme worth and perfection, your sin has been removed. Once for all. That's how good our high priest is. That's what Jesus is worth.

He's Gentle (5:2, 7-10)

To have a child with Zellweger syndrome, like our daughter, Hope, had, both parents must be carriers of the recessive gene trait. So after we had Hope, we knew that David and I are both carriers. Any child of ours would have a 25 percent chance of having the fatal syndrome. Matt had hit those 75 percent healthy odds, but Hope had not.

So after we had Hope, we took surgical steps to prevent a future pregnancy. Evidently, it didn't work. A year and a half after Hope died, I discovered that I was pregnant. We were shocked and afraid—afraid of what it would mean to perhaps love and lose a second child. We decided that before we told Matt and our parents and our friends about the pregnancy, we needed to understand the whole picture. We needed to know if the child I was carrying would also have a short and difficult life because of Zellweger syndrome like Hope had.

It was a hard day when David and I went to Vanderbilt Medical Center to undergo the prenatal testing. The test was uncomfortable physically. It was a placenta-sampling test, which means they plunged a big needle into my abdomen to extract a tiny piece of placenta. (Yes, it really hurt.) It was emotionally hard to walk back into the medical facility that brought back so many bittersweet memories of Hope's life and death, with thoughts that we might be plunged into that arena once again. But what added to the pain was the insensitive technician. I remember her chirping when she was finished, "Do you want a blue Band-Aid or a pink Band-Aid?" I knew she was trying to lighten the moment, but I thought to myself, *You just don't get it.* I wanted to say, "Do you have any idea why we are here? Do you understand what we are dealing with here?" Pink or blue seemed insignificant when for me the real issue was life or death.

But really she was rare among the medical people we dealt with. One of the most sensitive was the nurse assigned to me the morning I went into the hospital to be induced for Gabriel's birth. I don't remember her exact words, but she told me that she had given birth to a stillborn child. She knew what it was like to give birth when death, instead of life, was on the other side. Her experience equipped her to be gentle with me. And her understanding was a comfort to me.

This is a similar concept to what Hebrews 5:2 says about the priests of the Old Testament: "He is able to deal gently with those who are ignorant and are going astray, since he himself is subject to weakness." The ideal Levitical high priest was one of them. He dealt gently with sinners because he was also a sinner and understood their weakness from personal experience. He was subject to moral weakness, physical weakness, intellectual weakness, and emotional weakness. This helped him to deal with fellow sinners with compassion rather than condemnation.

Verses 7-9 give us a glimpse into the experience that enables Jesus to deal with us gently as our perfect High Priest.

> *During the days of Jesus' life on earth, he offered up prayers and petitions with loud cries and tears to the one who could save him from death, and he was heard because of his reverent submission. Although he was a son, he learned obedience from what he suffered and, once made perfect, he became the source of eternal salvation for all who obey him.* (HEBREWS 5:7-9)

Jesus is gentle with us because he has cried out to God like we have.

Do you know what it is to offer up prayers and petitions with loud cries and tears? I do. Do you know what it is to ask God for the strength to submit to his plan that brings you pain? So does Jesus. And that is why he is able to deal gently with those who are in the heat of the battle over obedience. Jesus is gentle with us because he has cried out to God like we have.

What does it mean that Jesus "learned obedience" from what he suffered? Was he in some way disobedient before?

No. This means that his obedience was tested and proven. He moved from obeying without any suffering to obeying through unspeakable suffering.[10] His was not automatic obedience. It was authentic obedience. This obedience was prayed for and begged for and cried out for and wept over with tears. Jesus learned through his own experience what it feels like for obedience to God to cost something—something painful.

Jesus learned through his own experience what it feels like for obedience to God to cost something—something painful.

Our perfect High Priest deals gently with those who are ignorant and have gone astray. Is that where you are today? To be ignorant means we just don't know where to start with God. To have gone astray means we've wandered away from God. Jesus will deal gently with us. He will be our compassionate High Priest who meets our needs. He will tenderly guide us into the presence of God so we can draw near.

He's Eternal (7:1-17)

I'm pretty good at figuring out who is guilty in a TV mystery show. Do you want to know my secret? When there is a pretty big guest star playing the assistant or the sister or a similar character, he or she is guilty. The more famous the actor, the more likely he or she did it—especially if that character seems to be unimportant at the beginning of the program.

Melchizedek is a little bit like that. He doesn't seem to be an important person in the Old Testament. He appears only once and is referred to just once more. You could hardly call his a starring role. But in terms of helping us understand the unique perfection of Christ's priesthood, he is a star; he gives us an important clue. He must be important if the writer of Hebrews gives him a whole chapter, right? Why would he do that?

Remember, before taking a tangent in chapters 5 and 6, the writer says that Jesus "was designated by God to be high priest in the order of Melchizedek" (5:10).

What does that mean? He is saying that Jesus is not a priest from the order of Levi, as all the other priests were. His priesthood is superior to that of Aaron and his descendants. He is a priest from the order of (or we might say, along the lines of) Melchizedek.

So if Melchizedek has been confusing to you like he has been to me, see him as a type of Christ. He was a man God designed as an illustration to help prepare the Jews for the real thing—the perfect High Priest, Jesus.

TYPES IN SCRIPTURE

A type is an impression made by a person, an object, or an event in the Old Testament that foreshadows the coming of the Messiah and gives a glimpse of who Jesus is and what he came to do.

PEOPLE AS TYPES OF CHRIST

Adam

Romans 5:14 describes Adam as "a pattern of the one to come," and 1 Corinthians 15:45 shows us the superiority of the fulfillment to the type: "It is written: 'The first man Adam became a living being'; the last Adam, a life-giving spirit."

Isaac

Isaac, the long-awaited child of promise, supernaturally born to Abraham and Sarah, is a type of Christ. Most compelling is the way he was offered as a sacrifice to God on Mount Moriah—a shadow of the sacrifice, some two thousand years later, when Jesus was offered as a sacrifice to God. Ephesians 5:2 says that "Christ loved us and gave himself up for us as a fragrant offering and sacrifice to God."

Joseph

Joseph said to his brothers, who had sold him into slavery, "You intended to harm me, but God intended it for good to accomplish what is now being done, the saving of many lives" (Genesis 50:20). Couldn't Jesus have said the same thing about those who nailed him to the cross?

Moses

As Moses was God's deliverer of the Israelites from Egypt, Christ is the greater deliverer. Galatians 1:3-4 tells us that Jesus "gave himself for our sins to rescue us from the present evil age, according to the will of our God and Father."

Jonah

Just as Jonah was sent to an unrepentant people, Jesus was sent to unrepentant Israel. Jesus compared the three days he would spend in the tomb before rising from the dead to the three days Jonah spent in the belly of the great fish: "A wicked and adulterous generation looks for a miraculous sign, but none will be given it except the sign of Jonah" (Matthew 16:4).

OTHER TYPES OF CHRIST

The Ark

Just as hiding in the ark saved Noah and his family from the wrath of God poured out on the earth through the Flood, so hiding in Christ provides salvation for us from the wrath of God.

Jacob's Ladder

In Genesis 28:12 we read about Jacob's vision of a ladder or stairway stretching from earth to heaven. Jesus presented himself as the reality to which the stairway pointed: "You shall see heaven open, and the angels of God ascending and descending on the Son of Man" (John 1:51).

The Bronze Snake

Numbers 21:9 describes a scene in the wilderness: "Moses made a bronze snake and put it up on a pole. Then when anyone was bitten by a snake and looked at the bronze snake, he lived." Jesus likened himself to that bronze snake: "Just as Moses lifted up the snake in the desert, so the Son of Man must be lifted up, that everyone who believes in him may have eternal life" (John 3:14-15).

The Temple

Jesus was the fulfillment of all that the Temple foreshadowed and symbolized. Just as the Temple was the place the Israelites attended to worship God properly and acceptably, now Jesus is the one we come to and through to worship God.

"The temple he had spoken of was his body. After he was raised from the dead, his disciples recalled what he had said. Then they believed the Scripture and the words that Jesus had spoken" (John 2:21-22).

Sacrifices

Most of the sacrificial offerings found throughout the Bible are types of Christ. For example, Leviticus 1:3 prescribes a sacrifice this way: "If the offering is a burnt offering from the herd, he is to offer a male without defect." Peter said that we've been redeemed "with the precious blood of Christ, a lamb without blemish or defect" (1 Peter 1:19).

Manna in the Wilderness

The bread provided for the children of Israel while they were wandering in the wilderness evidenced God's care and miraculous provision, but it was temporary. Jesus called himself the Bread of Life that would satisfy the soul eternally. In John 6:32 we read these words of Jesus: "I tell you the truth, it is not Moses who has given you the bread from heaven, but it is my Father who gives you the true bread from heaven."

What type of Christ from the Old Testament do you find referred to in the following verses in Hebrews?

3:2 (see Numbers 12:7)
4:16 (see Exodus 25:17-22 and Romans 3:25)
9:11 (see Exodus 40:2, 34)
9:12, 24 (see Leviticus 16:15-16)
10:10 (see Leviticus 1:2, 4)
13:11-12 (see Leviticus 4:2-3, 12)

It's important to recognize why the writer to the Hebrews brings Melchizedek up—in the only place he's mentioned in the New Testament. This writer is trying to convince the Hebrew people that someone (Jesus) who isn't even a descendant of Aaron is the perfect High Priest. The Hebrews all knew that someone couldn't be a priest unless he was from the tribe of Levi. So the writer to the Hebrews builds his case by reminding them that one thousand years before Aaron, there was a priest of God who was appointed by God and respected by Abraham, the father of their faith. He is saying that Jesus is not a priest by ancestry, like the Aaronic priests; he is a priest by appointment, like Melchizedek. Jesus is a priest because of who he is, not because of the family he came from.

When Hebrews 7:3 says that Melchizedek is "without father or mother, without genealogy," it doesn't mean that Melchizedek came from nowhere. It just means that in the Old Testament record there is nothing about his parents or origin. The point is that his genealogy is irrelevant to his priesthood.[11] Likewise, Jesus' genealogy is not significant in regard to his priesthood. The genealogy of Jesus is important, but not in regard to priesthood.

But the most important thing Melchizedek illustrates or shares in common with the priesthood of Jesus is that his priesthood is forever. When Melchizedek is described as being "without beginning of days or end of life" (Hebrews 7:3), the implication is not that he lives forever but that the order of priesthood in which he ministered is forever.

This stands in contrast to the Levitical priesthood, which was never meant to last forever and in fact has not lasted. The Levitical priesthood that was initiated with Aaron was dissolved when the Temple curtain was torn from top to bottom as Jesus paid with his own body the sacrifice to end all sacrifices on the cross (see Matthew 27:51).

So when we try to understand why Melchizedek is so important, what we need to understand clearly is this: Melchizedek is a type—a living illustration—that points to Jesus and helps us grasp the eternal permanance of Jesus' priesthood. This means that our salvation is as secure as Christ's priesthood is indestructable. "Because Jesus lives forever, he has a permanent priesthood" (7:24). [12] Long after everyone you depend on in this life is dead and gone, Jesus will be alive and serving as your priest in the presence of God. When your future seems uncertain, rest in knowing that the priesthood of Jesus on your behalf is "forever, in the order of Melchizedek" (7:17).

He's Able to Save (7:25)

> *He is able to save completely those who come to God through him.*
> (HEBREWS 7:25)

In the NASB, 7:25 reads, "He is able also to save *forever* those who draw near to God through Him, since He always lives to make intercession for them" (emphasis added).

This verse tells us why this whole explanation that Jesus is the perfect High Priest should matter to us. This is the "so what" of the superior priesthood of Jesus: He is able to save completely and forever.

The priests couldn't cleanse the people of sin, no matter how much they wanted to, no matter how many animals they slaughtered. The relief the animal sacrifices brought from sin's guilt and power was temporary and limited. Today's sacrifice took care of today's sins, but tomorrow's sins sent them on another trek to the Temple.

But Jesus is not only willing to save us from the guilt and penalty of our sins; he is able. Jesus is able to remove our sin and shame completely and forever. He can do what no human priest or any other person or philosophy or prophet can do. He doesn't just cover our sins—he cleanses us of them. He takes them away.

Jesus is the only priest who is able to save. Jesus can save anyone. Jesus saves permanently.

> You don't have to be an insider with connections to gain access to God. There is only one connection that counts.

Whom does he save? Those who draw near to God through him. You don't need a backstage pass. You don't have to be an insider with connections to gain access to God. There is only one connection that counts. A day is coming when your answer to one question will be the only thing that matters: What have you done with Jesus?

Jesus actually told us about that day. He said, "Not everyone who says to me, 'Lord, Lord,' will enter the kingdom of heaven, but only he who does the will of my Father who is in heaven. Many will say to me on that day, 'Lord, Lord, did we not prophesy in your name, and in your name drive out demons and perform many miracles?' Then I will tell them plainly, 'I never knew you. Away from me, you evildoers!'" (Matthew 7:21-23).

Who are these people who will not be saved? These are people who want to use Jesus but don't want Jesus. They don't want to love him or live with him. They don't want to hide themselves in him and depend on him. These are people who have been invited to draw near but have said, "No thanks, I'm not in the market. That may work for some people, but it's not for me. I don't need that."

Don't believe the lie that there are many paths to God, as if deciding it is so could make it so.

And if that is you, I have to ask: Do you really think you've got what it takes to stand before a holy God with no priest to represent you and explain to God why you're deserving of his heaven?

Don't believe the lie that there are many paths to God, as if deciding it is so could make it so. It sounds appealing and accommodating and reasonable. But to place your faith in that idea, to take your chances on it means that you never give yourself to Jesus, never believe that he is the one way God has provided and prescribed for you to draw near to him.

To draw near to God, you need no other qualification except faith in God's Son. He is able to save all, but not all will be saved, because not all will choose to draw near to God through him.

He Intercedes (7:25)

He always lives to intercede for them. (HEBREWS 7:25)

Just as we can't save ourselves, we can't keep ourselves saved. And just as Jesus has the power to save us, he has the power to keep us.

Our future salvation depends on the active work of Christ as our High Priest forever and ever, not just his past work on the cross or our past decisions or commitments. This very day we are being saved by the eternal intercession of Jesus.[13] Today, Jesus is praying for us. That's one of the things he lives for.

He Meets Our Need (7:26-28)

Such a high priest meets our need. (HEBREWS 7:26)

To be a Christian is not just to have Jesus as your example. To be a Christian is to be in Christ, to be united with him, to have him as your substitute, your advocate, your priest. He is your advocate in the only court that counts. Jesus is your connection for access into the very presence of God.

So what is keeping you from drawing near? Do you feel unworthy? You don't have to be worthy. Your High Priest is worthy and has covered you in his inestimable worth so that you will be able to draw near.

Do you fear having all your weaknesses and failures thrown back in your face? When you draw near to the throne through Jesus, you will not find a throne of judgment. His is a throne of mercy and grace. You will find mercy so that you will not be met with the hostility and punishment you deserve. Instead, you'll be showered with grace you don't deserve and could never earn.

You'll be accepted, not berated; loved, not lectured.

"Let us then approach the throne of grace with confidence, so that we may receive mercy and find grace to help us in our time of need" (Hebrews 4:16). Our priest, Jesus, has made this possible. And entering into his presence is the something better you've been longing for out there on your own.

You'll be accepted, not berated; loved, not lectured.

Jesus meets our every need. So let's draw near.

Jesus gives us the access to God we could never get on our own.

CHAPTER 5

how can you know that your faith is for real?

HEBREWS 5:11–6:20

TODAY IS A BIG day in my life. Or more correctly, twenty years ago today was a big day in my life. Twenty years ago today while I was at lunch at the Steak & Ale restaurant in Waco, Texas, a group of men who worked at the same company I did walked past our table and spoke to the group of women I was having lunch with. I turned to one of the men and said, "I don't think we've met. I'm Nancy Jinks." And he said, "I'm Dave Guthrie."

On October 18, 1985, I met David. On October 18, 1986, we got married. And in between was the period of time when we were figuring out if what we had was the real thing, if we wanted to make a commitment to spend the rest of our lives together.

We had been dating only a few months when I found myself wishing he would ask me to marry him. And one day I realized that I had not made "the list." You know what I mean. Always before when it came to guys, I had made "the list" detailing the positives about him and our relationship on one side and the negatives on the other—always looking for the positives to outweigh the negatives or to figure out if I could live with the negatives. I realized that here I was, wanting David to ask me to marry him, and I hadn't even made the list. So I went off by myself with my notebook and pen and sat down to make the list.

But I quickly realized I didn't need to make a list. There were no lingering questions. He was the one. Perhaps that's when I realized that all those people who had said that when you meet the right one "you'll know" were right. I knew.

But knowing wasn't completely subjective. I had observed him carefully. He was a man of faith and integrity and character. He was interesting and smart and funny. He accepted my weaknesses while appreciating my strengths. We shared the same values and dreams and faith. And so even though I didn't write out the list that day, I could have.

Do you think it is the same way with faith? Can we just expect to "know" that the faith we claim is real, that it will last forever? Or are there some specific objective realities in a person's life that give evidence that his or her faith is real? Most important, how can we know that our faith is for real?

Paul instructed us in 2 Corinthians 13:5, "Test yourselves to see if you are in the faith; examine yourselves! Or do you not recognize this about yourselves, that Jesus Christ is in you—unless indeed you fail the test?" (NASB).

Chapters 5 and 6 in Hebrews help us with this question, because the writer does not want us to live wondering and wavering. His aim in his warnings as well as his exhortations is to encourage us. We see it in 6:18-19: God confirmed his promise so that "we who have fled to take hold of the hope offered to us *may be greatly encouraged.* We have this hope as an anchor for the soul, firm and secure" (emphasis added).

If you find yourself wondering if your faith is for real, if you live with a sense of uncertainty about whether or not you have really come to know Jesus in a saving way, the message of Hebrews 5 and 6 is for you.

Likewise, for those who have assumed they're fine, assumed that their faith is for real while their lives do not reflect what this passage says is true of people with real faith, then this passage is for them, too. It serves as a warning or as a wake-up call.

This passage outlines some solid specifics about how a person with real faith lives—how she thinks, how she feels, what she does. So if you have been in a place of wondering if your faith is for real, this passage offers clarity and confidence. And if you have had a false sense of comfort, this passage will show you that, too.

If you have been in a place of wondering if your faith is for real, this passage offers clarity and confidence. And if you have had a false sense of comfort, this passage will show you that, too.

You may have noticed that in the previous chapter we were cruising along in chapter 5 of Hebrews and then we jumped to chapter 7, all about Melchizedek, skipping 5:11–6:20. Why did we do that? Because that is what the writer did, in a sense. This passage is like an aside, a very important aside. It begins with this: "Concerning him we have much to say, and it is hard to explain, since you have become dull of hearing" (NASB).

Who is *him*? Melchizedek.

In the previous verse (5:10), the writer says that Jesus is a "priest in the order of Melchizedek." And it is almost as if he realizes, in a bit of frustration perhaps, that the people reading his letter aren't going to understand what he is talking about when he says, "in the order of Melchizedek." It is as if he is going along, teaching about Jesus as the perfect High Priest, when he realizes he can't assume they understand the implications of what he is saying.

He realizes that many of those who will hear his letter read to them have not grown up enough spiritually to get his point and grasp his explanation. They're still stuck on the basics of Judaism—all of the signs and symbols and shadows that point to Christ. These are the "elementary teachings" referred to in 6:1. These important teachings point to Christ, but the problem is that these people are still stuck on the basics. They haven't matured past the picture book that points to Christ, so they can't yet embrace the full reality of Christ himself.

ELEMENTARY TEACHINGS ABOUT CHRIST

I had always assumed that the list of "elementary teachings about Christ" referred to in 6:1-2 (repentance from dead works, faith in God, baptism instructions, the laying on of hands, the resurrection of the dead, and eternal judgment) were basic Christian doctrine. But I've come to realize that this is a list of basics from Judaism that pointed toward Christ but were not the fullness of Christ.

Arthur W. Pink writes, "The apostle is not contrasting two different stages of Christianity, an infantile and a mature; rather is he opposing, once more, the substance over against the shadows. He continues to press upon the Hebrews their need of forsaking the visible for the invisible, the typical for the antitypical. . . . They had not yet clearly grasped the fact that Judaism was but a temporary economy. . . . Now that He had come and finished His work the types had served their purpose, and the shadows were replaced by the Substance."[14]

R. Kent Hughes writes, "The six facets of 'the elementary teachings about Christ' listed in verses 1-3 outline the primitive catechism used in Jewish churches to induct converts. Thus we get an intimate glimpse of 'the basics,' the foundation you would have been taught before being baptized and accepted into a Jewish church 2,000 years ago."[15]

John Piper says: "This list . . . is made up of foundational Old Testament and Jewish truths and practices that the readers probably built on when they were converted. . . . When these readers were evangelized and converted, these things, it seems, had been made foundational as a way of helping them understand the work of Christ. Christ is the goal and fulfillment of all these things. So when verse 1 says they should leave the 'elementary teachings about Christ' (or literally: 'the word of the beginning of Christ'), what I think it means is that they should not occupy themselves so much with the pre-Christian foundational preparations for Christ that they neglect the glory of the gospel and how to use it to grow into maturity and holiness."[16]

In this passage we sense the writer's frustration that these people have allowed themselves to become spiritually lazy. They are spiritual infants despite having known Christ for many years. And everybody knows that something is terribly wrong with a baby who doesn't grow.

A CRAVING FOR GOD'S WORD

> *We have much to say about this, but it is hard to explain because you are slow to learn. In fact, though by this time you ought to be teachers, you need someone to teach you the elementary truths of God's word all over again. You need milk, not solid food! Anyone who lives on milk, being still an infant, is not acquainted with the teaching about righteousness. But solid food is for the mature, who by constant use have trained themselves to distinguish good from evil. Therefore let us leave the elementary teachings about Christ and go on to maturity, not laying again the foundation of repentance from acts that lead to death, and of faith in God, instruction about baptisms, the laying on of hands, the resurrection of the dead, and eternal judgment. And God permitting, we will do so.* (HEBREWS 5:11–6:3)

The first indicator of authentic faith is a growing relationship with God through his Word.

Take It In

> *Anyone who lives on milk, being still an infant, is not acquainted with the teaching about righteousness.* (HEBREWS 5:13)

The writer is using the metaphor of food to illustrate the nourishing power of God's Word. Just as babies begin with milk and move on to solid food, so believers begin with the basics that are easy to digest, and then move on to more challenging—but also more rewarding—truths.

But the writer realizes that some of us may have known Christ for decades, and yet we are still spiritual infants.

If your faith is real, it should be growing. The growth may not be in

If your faith is real, it should be growing. The growth may not be in dramatic spurts, and you may still have a long way to go, but ongoing growth is a critical sign of spiritual life.

dramatic spurts, and you may still have a long way to go, but ongoing growth is a critical sign of spiritual life.

Are you growing in your understanding of who God is and how he works? Are you growing in your appetite for God's Word and his ways? Are you growing in Christlikeness?

If we find that we have no appetite for God's Word, no delight in chewing on it, no desire to grow in our understanding and enjoyment of all the riches available in Christ, then we have cause to wonder if we have really joined ourselves in a love relationship with him.

Imagine that you go through a marriage ceremony with someone, but you never live together. You never talk to each other. You never connect in any meaningful way. Could you really say you are married?

Similarly, even if you went through a religious ceremony or walked down an aisle at some point, if you never want to spend time with God and communicate with him to hear his heart and share yours with him, does it make sense to say you are connected to him in a genuine, meaningful way?

Genuine faith makes us hungry for the Word of God. Because we love him, we want to listen to him. We want to feast on his Word because it nourishes us and because we want to grow.

Of course, just as we go through times when our feelings fluctuate in human relationships, most of us go through seasons of dryness in our times in God's Word—when it doesn't seem to speak or when we simply aren't interested in listening. Even here we find a revealer of genuine faith. When faith is real, we long for a restored relationship, we long to hear him speak to us again, and we pursue him until we can hear him.

Give It Out

By this time you ought be to be teachers. (HEBREWS 5:12)

What does the writer mean? Does he really think we all should be teaching a class? Well, yes and no.

To be a teacher doesn't necessarily mean we have official teaching roles. Or it might. What it does mean is that we are exploring scriptural truth. We are wrestling with its implications in our lives and in the world, and because it is so interesting and so important, we can't help talking about it. We not only take it in, we give it out.

We all know that it is one thing to kind of understand something when we hear it or read it. But it is another whole level of understanding to get it enough to explain it to somebody else. For that, we have to have a firm grasp of the big picture. The studying to give it out and the act of giving it out are what increases and solidifies our understanding.

Last week Matt had a test in his biology honors class. I noticed that he quickly abandoned studying and turned on a video game, so I suggested that he let me quiz him. He put up a real fuss about that. He didn't want to do it. I figured out that his frustration level was high because he just wasn't getting the material, and it frustrated him even more that I was asking him questions he couldn't answer.

So we persevered together. We discussed the material and tried to simplify it and make sense of it, digging deeper into the concepts we found difficult to understand and attempting to explain them to each other. He ended up doing better on that test than he has done so far in the class, and we learned a lesson in the value of "giving out" what we want to learn well.

We can hear or read something and forget it so quickly. But when we talk through and write down what we have heard, it becomes much more solidified in our hearts and minds.

If we just hear truth, but we never write it out or wrestle with it, if we never try to repeat it or explain it to someone else, we never really own it. It will leave us as quickly as it came. And we will find ourselves needing to learn the "elementary truths" over and over again.

If we just hear truth, but we never write it out or wrestle with it, if we never try to repeat it or explain it to someone else, we never really own it. It will leave us as quickly as it came.

There are spiritual treasures waiting for us in God's Word. We can never exhaust the beauty and profundity and solidity of the truth in God's Word. It is not dry and boring. It is not just for Sunday. It is not just for theologians and preachers. It is for us. Don't settle for repeating kindergarten over and over again. Grow up in God's Word. Take it in and give it out. Move from the milk to the meat, and enjoy it richly.

Live It Out

When our faith is genuine, we not only give it out, we live it out.

> *Solid food is for the mature, who by constant use have trained themselves to distinguish good from evil.* (HEBREWS 5:14)

What does this mean, that "by constant use" we train ourselves to "distinguish good from evil"?

We have a list of dos and don'ts from God in the Ten Commandments that show us how to live. So we don't have to wonder if it is okay to steal from our friend's purse or sleep with a man who is not our husband or covet someone else's bank account balance.

But when it comes to deciding whether or not to watch *Desperate Housewives,* whether to drive a hybrid or an SUV, whether to spank or use time-outs, whether to have a glass of wine or take a pass, we need discernment. We can't depend on our natural instincts. At least we can't when we are babies in faith. But as we mature, as our minds are renewed, our desires are retrained, our values and priorities are replaced, and we find that our natural instincts are reshaped.

> As we delight ourselves in the Lord, he gives us the desires of our hearts, and we begin to find that what we want most is what is pleasing to God.

Discernment develops as we nourish ourselves with the Word of God. It becomes a part of us and teaches us how to distinguish good from evil. What used to be acceptable to us becomes distasteful, and we don't want it anymore. We have new appetites. As we delight ourselves in the Lord, he gives us the desires of our hearts, and we begin to find that what we want most is what is pleasing to God.

In this way we not only take in and give out God's Word, we live out God's Word. God's Word changes us on the inside, and it changes what we want and how we live.

Do you have a craving to take in more of God's Word? Have you discovered the pleasure in giving it out? Would anyone around you see that you are living it out?

CONFIDENCE TO LIVE WHAT YOU BELIEVE

> *It is impossible for those who have once been enlightened, who have tasted the heavenly gift, who have shared in the Holy Spirit, who have tasted the goodness of the word of God and the powers of the coming age, if they fall away, to be brought back to repentance, because to their loss they are crucifying the Son of God all over again and subjecting him to public disgrace.* (HEBREWS 6:4-6)

Do Not Fall Away

This can be a very disconcerting set of verses. If we're not careful, we can read into these verses that a person can have real faith and then lose it, and then be barred from restoration to real faith.

But that is not what these verses are saying. Such an interpretation does not fit with numerous other verses in Hebrews and elsewhere in Scripture that make it clear that those who genuinely come to faith in Christ can never be separated from Christ. Those who are adopted by him can never be disowned by him.

So what do these verses mean? What is this warning, and whom is it for? Throughout the book of Hebrews there are warnings against drifting and dullness, and here we find a warning against a false sense of security.

The people described here have "been enlightened . . . tasted the heavenly gift . . . shared in the Holy Spirit . . . tasted the goodness of the word of God and the powers of the coming age." At first blush, this can sound like the description of a real believer. But it isn't.

Sometimes when I'm at a party I pick up some little finger food that looks good and I take a bite, only to find it falls into that category of "looks better than it tastes" or simply "not worth the calories." And I've been known to discreetly spit out the bite I took into my napkin and throw it away. I tasted it and decided it wasn't for me. Please don't report me to Miss Manners.

OUR SECURITY AS BELIEVERS

Numerous verses in Hebrews give us confidence and assurance that once we have placed our faith in Christ and become a part of his family, he will not disown us or abandon us.

- In Hebrews 3:3-6, Christ is compared to the maker and master of a house, and Christians are compared to the house itself. Verse 6 says, "Christ was faithful as a Son over His house—whose house we are, if we hold fast our confidence and the boast of our hope firm until the end" (NASB). It doesn't say that we *will* become his house if we hold fast to our hope; it says that we *are* his house if we hold fast to our hope. So holding fast is not the cause of our being Christ's house but the proof of it. This security is not a result of our own ability to persevere. Our perseverance is the result of this security provided for us in Christ.
- Hebrews 3:14 says, "We have become partakers of Christ, if we hold fast the beginning of our assurance firm until the end" (NASB). It doesn't say that we *will* become partakers of Christ if we are able to work up enough endurance to keep holding on but that we *have* become partakers, evidenced by the fact that we hold fast. Another way to say it is that our holding on to Christ is proof or evidence that we belong to Christ, not the cause of our belonging to Christ.
- Hebrews 6:9 warns against drifting away from God. But then it says, "But, beloved, we are convinced of better things concerning you, and things that accompany salvation" (NASB). The "better things . . . that accompany salvation" are the opposite of drifting away. The better things are perseverance in faith and patient obedience. The gift of salvation includes the security and eternity of that salvation, and it cannot be taken away.

Other verses that confirm our security as believers include John 10:27-28; Romans 8:30, 35-39; 1 Corinthians 1:8; 2 Corinthians 1:22; and 1 Thessalonians 5:23-24.

It is possible to "taste the heavenly gift," to "taste the goodness of the word of God," to be "enlightened" by the light of Christ that spills into your life—and even benefit from the work of the Holy Spirit in this world—but never consume it, swallow it, or commit to it. It is possible to nibble at the edges of life in Christ and decide, "I don't really like this. It is not for me. It's not worth it. I don't want it." This is the person this passage is talking about.

It is possible to nibble at the edges of life in Christ and decide, "I don't really like this. It is not for me. It's not worth it. I don't want it."

The Holy Spirit will give us a taste of the richness of Christ, but he will not make us eat.

This passage is not talking about believers who are in danger of losing their salvation. It is about unbelievers who are in danger of losing their opportunity to receive salvation.[17]

Tasting is the first step toward eating, but tasting is not the same as eating. You have to chew and swallow and digest. Tasting is just the first step.

But I suppose there is a bit of danger in tasting too. Because it is one thing to never taste of the truth and richness found in Christ and be uninitiated to his goodness. But it is another thing to take a taste of him, enjoy his light and his goodness, and see his power at work . . . and then walk away.

The writer of Hebrews says about these people that it is "impossible" (6:4) for them to be brought back to repentance. What does he mean?

He is talking about those who get a taste of who Jesus is and what he offers up close, those who experience personally some of the joy and the blessings he gives and the hope he offers. With that experience and knowledge, if they decide they don't want him, salvation is forever out of their reach.

It is impossible not because God withdraws the offer but because they have rejected his offer.

But falling away is not a possibility for someone with real faith. If your faith is real, you will not fall away. Not because you are strong or because your faith is strong but because God has his firm grip on you and he will not let you go. You will remain in him because you are his forever, and he will never allow you to fall away.

If your faith is real, you will not fall away. Not because you are strong or because your faith is strong but because God has his firm grip on you and he will not let go. You will remain in him because you are his forever, and he will never allow you to fall away.

Produce Spiritual Fruit

Rather than falling away, those with genuine faith are fruitful. Rather than having barrenness or meaninglessness in their lives, there is a flowering, a fullness, a crop of fruit that can't grow out of a dead spirit. There is love that can only flow from a heart that has experienced the love of Christ, and diligence that is not dependent on human will or endurance.

Land that drinks in the rain often falling on it and that produces a crop useful to those for whom it is farmed receives the blessing of God. But land that produces thorns and thistles is worthless and is in danger of being cursed. In the end it will be burned. (HEBREWS 6:7-8)

What does it mean to produce a crop or bear spiritual fruit? Galatians 5:22-23 tells us clearly what spiritual fruit looks like in a real believer's life. "The fruit of the Spirit is love, joy, peace, patience, kindness, goodness, faithfulness, gentleness and self-control."

"But," you say, "I'm just not naturally a gentle person" or "I'm not a naturally kind person." Well, that's the point! The evidence that the Holy Spirit is active in our lives is that he supernaturally produces this kind of fruit in us, so that we no longer do what comes naturally.

Is the fruit of the Spirit evident in your life? Are you marked by an ever-increasing measure of love, joy, peace, patience, kindness, goodness, faithfulness, gentleness, and self-control?

Love Others Well

Even though we speak like this, dear friends, we are confident of better things in your case—things that accompany salvation. God is not unjust; he will not forget your work and the love you have shown him as you have helped his people and continue to help them. (HEBREWS 6:9-10)

God sees and does not forget what we do for others out of love for Christ. These works of love are not what save us or keep us saved, but they are evidence that we are saved. If we have been changed by Christ in a way that causes us to care for others as Jesus would, it points to faith that is genuine.

Show Diligence to the End

> *We want each of you to show this same diligence to the very end, in order to make your hope sure. We do not want you to become lazy, but to imitate those who through faith and patience inherit what has been promised.* (HEBREWS 6:11-12)

Just when we think the writer is beginning to focus on works, we find he has brought us back to the subject of faith. What does it mean to "show this same diligence to the very end, in order to make your hope sure"? He is telling us to be diligent and purposeful in putting our hope solely in God and not in the things of the world. He is encouraging us not to get sidetracked along the way, even in doing good things. He is reminding us that there is an inheritance waiting for us but that we have to stay patient, willing to wait for God to fulfill his promises to us.

Do you wonder if your faith is real? If it is, it will change how you live. You will not fall away. Your life will bear unmistakable spiritual fruit—not just surfacy niceness, but eternal spiritual fruit that is supernatural in origin. You will love others well, overflowing from the love you've experienced in Jesus. And you will be diligent in your life of faith, patiently waiting for all of God's promises to be realized. Your hope in Christ will give you the confidence to live what you believe.

COURAGE TO BELIEVE WHAT GOD HAS SAID

Waiting Patiently

> *When God made his promise to Abraham, since there was no one greater for him to swear by, he swore by himself, saying, "I will surely bless you and give you many descendants." And so after waiting patiently, Abraham received what was promised.* (HEBREWS 6:13-15)

Abraham believed. What did he believe? He believed God's promises. When God told Abraham that he would give him many descendants, Abraham believed it. But he had to wait an awfully long time to see the fulfillment of God's promises.

It's hard to wait, isn't it? We want what we want, here and now. God has promised us a home and an inheritance and a future in which there will be no more tears and no more sorrow. It sounds so good to us. We want it, and we want it now. But if our faith is real, we believe in these promises of God and we are willing to wait patiently.

If you find you don't really believe that what God has promised to you is worth waiting for, and if you find you are not willing to wait patiently but demand to have your desires met here and now in this life with what this world has to offer, then obviously you've made your choice.

But if you want to turn away from grabbing at this world with all the gusto you can, it is still not too late . . . there is something more solid and sure to grab on to.

Taking Hold

> *Because God wanted to make the unchanging nature of his purpose very clear to the heirs of what was promised, he confirmed it with an oath. God did this so that, by two unchangeable things in which it is impossible for God to lie, we who have fled to take hold of the hope offered to us may be greatly encouraged. We have this hope as an anchor for the soul, firm and secure. It enters the inner sanctuary behind the curtain, where Jesus, who went before us, has entered on our behalf. He has become a high priest forever, in the order of Melchizedek.* (HEBREWS 6:17-20)

"We who have fled to take hold of the hope." Is this you? Have you fled away from human answers and worldly wisdom and commonly accepted antidotes to the pain of this life, toward Jesus? Have you taken hold of the hope he offers you?

The hope Jesus offers is not unbridled optimism despite evident realities. It is not escapist denial. This hope is centered in the reality that Jesus is everything we need in this life and the next.

Many of you have done what I did nineteen years ago today. You stood at an altar and made promises and believed the promises made to you by a man you loved. You staked your earthly happiness on the promises of another person. Today I want to invite you to stake your eternal happiness not on the promises of a person but on the promises of God.

But even as I use this illustration of wedding-day promises, some of you are troubled. Because some of you know what it is to be on the other end of broken promises. You know what it is to experience the devastating disappointment of being abandoned by someone who said he or she would always be there. Likewise, some of you know what it is to find that you were unable to live up to the promises you made. You intended to, but you couldn't.

So what makes the promises of God different? What makes them secure enough to stake your life on, sure enough to grab on to and depend on? These verses tell us that God wants us to be encouraged and confident. He wants our lives to be anchored securely in what he has promised us. He wants us to know that he will never change his mind about his purposes for us.

He wants to increase our courage so we will have what it takes to grab hold of his promises in a world of broken promises.

Hebrews 6:17 says he confirmed his promise with an oath. Why did he do this? Is it because his word wasn't good enough? No. God cannot lie.

God didn't have to swear by an oath. He did that to accommodate us, because he knows that we know what it is like to be on the losing end of broken promises. He wants to increase our courage so we will have what it takes to grab hold of his promises in a world of broken promises.

God swears on the highest, most honorable name he can swear on—his own. His promise and his oath are meant to give us the deep confidence that we will inherit all he has promised us in Jesus.

Our security is not dependent on our ability to keep our promises to God. We want to, but we are made of flesh and we are unfaithful. He will keep his promises to us, and that is enough—if we will grab on to those promises and claim them as our own through faith. It is up to us to grab on to the hope God offers. But to take that leap of faith can be terrifying.

A couple of years ago I spoke at a women's retreat outside Dallas. I had flight problems, so I missed the morning sessions. When I got there, all the women were out enjoying the camp for the afternoon, including the zip line. Do you know what that is? The participant climbs a tower about five stories high and hooks herself on. Then she steps off the tower and flies through the air for the length of about three football fields while hanging on to this zip line, strapped in with a series of harnesses and hooks.

Well, I wanted to enter into what these women were doing and just have fun with them, so I didn't want to say, "No, I'm too chicken to do the zip line." So I got in line with them and said, "Sure I'll do it!" But honestly, I wasn't sure I could.

When I finally made my way up the tower and onto the ledge, I probably would have turned around and said, "Forget it" if there hadn't been a long line of people on the stairs behind me. I didn't want to make a total fool of myself. So I sat down on the ledge, and with my heart pounding, full of fear, I pushed off—screaming. But my scream of fear lasted only a moment, giving way to shrieks of laughter. It was so much fun, I couldn't wait to do it again!

Sitting on that ledge, I had to decide whether or not I believed the ropes and belts and clips would hold me and carry me safely to the end of the line. I had seen them hold other women. I chose to believe they would hold me, too. So I took a deep breath and pushed off.

That is what I want to invite you to do if you have never done it—take a deep breath and push off. And if you have only done it one time—the time you look back on as the time you trusted Christ to save you, I want to invite you to grab on to him again in a new and perhaps deeper way. Trust him with everything you are and everything you have and everyone you love. You can trust that the promises of God are strong and sure enough to hold you.

Trusting in God's promises is the thrill of a lifetime and evidence that the faith you claim is for real. Let your confidence in his promises give you the courage to grab on to the hope he offers. He will not let you fall.

Jesus instills an appetite for God's Word and confidence to trust God's promises.

CHAPTER 6

how will you get rid of your guilt?

HEBREWS 8:1–10:18

YOU KNOW WHAT I hate? I hate it when I get a new outfit and the first time I wear it I spill something on it that leaves a spot that won't come out.

That's what happened to the blue shirt I'm wearing today. I wore it one time and dropped some salad dressing on it, and now there's a spot that will not go away. Bummer.

I almost just got rid of the shirt. But I decided I would keep it to wear under sweaters because it has a good collar. So that's what I'm doing today. I've covered it up, so no one who's looking at me will even know it has a spot on it.

But I know.

No matter how well the sweater covers up the spot, I know that the stain is there, taunting me, reminding me of what a messy eater I am. I see the spot and I'm disgusted by my childish inability to get through a meal without being left with a permanent reminder of it.

The spot also taunts me by reminding me that I was not given the laundress gene. Plenty of pink undershirts, shrunken sweaters, and bleach-spotted darks testify to this.

Fortunately I have a husband who gives me grace and who is even willing to do the laundry himself. (Although I sometimes think this is because he's tired of my ruining his stuff. . . .) Anyway, don't look too closely at the Guthrie family wardrobe, okay?

The reality is, all of us have spots and stains that we're ashamed of—not on our clothing but on the inside of our lives. We've done things we're not proud of; we have tendencies we're ashamed of. There are blots on our record that we have done our best to cover up.

Honestly there are things I've done that make me wince when I remember them. It is almost as if I sense the memory entering my frontal lobe and I do my best to slam the door on it so I won't have to think about it and feel the pain of regret again.

Is there anything more painful than regret? Most of us who have been around for any length of time have plenty of it—relationship blunders we're sorry for, attitudes we're ashamed of, hurts we've inflicted on others, anguish we've brought upon ourselves through self-centered, impulsive choices. We all have those things we've done that we are relieved no one can see on the surface, things we've tried to hide, hoping no one will notice.

And yet they eat away at us on the inside. Many of us carry around a heavy load of guilt and shame.

So what are we going to do? Are we destined to live forever pulling a sweater over our lives in an effort to cover up the mistakes we've made, the messes we keep making? How are we going to get rid of our guilt?

In Hebrews 8–10 we see that God has provided a way for us to get rid of our very real guilt so that we might draw near to him and know him.

From the beginning of time, God knew that we would need a real remedy for our guilt, even though we do our best to cover it up. That's what Adam and Eve did in the Garden. Genesis 3:7 says that after they ate the fruit, "the eyes of both of them were opened, and they realized they were naked; so they sewed fig leaves together and made coverings for themselves."

We come from a long line of sinners who want to pull a sweater over their shame.

So what did God do to deal with Adam and Eve's stained record? Genesis 3:21 tells us that "the LORD God made garments of skin for Adam and his wife and clothed them." An animal was killed so that Adam and Eve could be covered. Ever since the beginning of time, the remedy for our guilt has always required that blood be shed.

The old covenant fulfilled its purpose, in that it showed us our sin and our complete inability to be pleasing to God on our own.

God instituted the old covenant with blood, and the Old Testament sacrificial system was awash in blood. But the sacrificial system was never meant to last forever. It was the picture book for beginners in God, instituted to point us to and prepare us for the new covenant and the perfect sacrifice. Hebrews 8–10 helps us to see just how much better the new covenant and the perfect sacrifice really are.

But before we can see how the new covenant is better, we have to understand what the old covenant was. When the writer of Hebrews talks about the old covenant, he is talking about the Mosaic covenant—Israel had to obey the laws Moses had brought down from Mount Sinai, and many of the blessings promised them were conditioned on that obedience.

God set the standard in the law—but the children of Israel were people just like us. They couldn't live up to the standard. They couldn't obey. They were destined to fail in living up to their part of the covenant. The old covenant fulfilled its purpose, in that it showed us our sin and our complete inability to be pleasing to God on our own.

A BETTER COVENANT

The writer of Hebrews quotes the prophet Jeremiah in Hebrews 8:8-11:

> *God found fault with the people and said: "The time is coming, declares the Lord, when I will make a new covenant with the house of Israel and with the house of Judah. It will not be like the covenant I made with their forefathers when I took them by the hand to lead them out of Egypt, because they did not remain faithful to my covenant, and I turned away from them, declares the Lord. This is the covenant I will make with the house of Israel after that time,*

declares the Lord. I will put my laws in their minds and write them on their hearts. I will be their God, and they will be my people. No longer will a man teach his neighbor, or a man his brother, saying, 'Know the Lord,' because they will all know me, from the least of them to the greatest."

WHAT IS A COVENANT?

According to the encyclopedia, a covenant is "an agreement or mutual obligation, contracted with solemnity."[18] But when it comes to God's making a covenant with humans, there is a problem with that definition. God does not negotiate with anyone as to the degree of their allegiance to him. He comes to us and offers a covenant relationship with the terms already decided. Through covenants God obligated himself to people with solemn promises:

- To Noah: "I establish my covenant with you: Never again will all life be cut off by the waters of a flood; never again will there be a flood to destroy the earth" (Genesis 9:11).
- To Abraham: "I will confirm my covenant between me and you and will greatly increase your numbers. . . . This is my covenant with you: You will be the father of many nations" (Genesis 17:2, 4).
- To Moses: "I am making a covenant with you. Before all your people I will do wonders never before done in any nation in all the world" (Exodus 34:10).
- To David: "I have made a covenant with my chosen one, I have sworn to David my servant, 'I will establish your line forever and make your throne firm through all generations'" (Psalm 89:3-4).

WHAT IS THE OLD COVENANT?

God made this covenant with Israel in the days of Moses, when he gave them the Law in context of his loving relationship with them: "I am the LORD your God, who brought you out of Egypt, out of the land of slavery" (Exodus 20:2). The old covenant was based on mercy and provided for forgiveness. It had divine promises, warnings, and commandments. Its most basic requirement was single-minded devotion to God alone.

In Exodus 19:8 we read that the people accepted the covenant: "We will do everything the Lord has said."

Through the Law (or the Ten Commandments), God summarized his will for man on stone tablets. The old covenant not only spelled out the law of God; it expressed God's mercy, forgiveness, and love (see Exodus 34:6-7), and it called the people to faith demonstrated by obedience (see Numbers 14:11; Hebrews 3:19). But while the terms and commandments were not faulty, the people's hearts were. The weakness of the old covenant was that it wasn't accompanied by an outpouring of God's Spirit to bring an internal change of heart.

WHAT IS THE NEW COVENANT?

The new covenant is also based on mercy and provides for forgiveness. It, too, has divine promises, warnings, and commandments. And once again, its most basic requirement is single-hearted devotion to God alone. So what makes it new? The prophet Jeremiah told us what would be new (which the writer to the Hebrews quotes): "'The time is coming,' declares the Lord, 'when I will make a new covenant with the house of Israel and with the house of Judah. It will not be like the covenant I made with their forefathers. . . . I will put my law in their minds and write it on their hearts. I will be their God, and they will be my people'" (Jeremiah 31:31-33).

The new covenant is purchased by the blood of Christ, effected by the Spirit of Christ, and appropriated by faith in Christ. According to the new covenant arrangements, everything God demands of us, he also provides for us—freely and forever, through the finished work of Christ on the cross. Through the new covenant, the Spirit of God overcomes our rebellion and resistance so that we can have an internal change of heart toward God.

God did not start over with the new covenant but instead brought the old covenant to perfection. The role of the old covenant was to foreshadow the important work Christ would do and point us toward our need for something better. This is what Hebrews 8:6 speaks of: Christ "is also the mediator of a better covenant, which has been enacted on better promises" (NASB). This is why Paul wrote in 2 Corinthians 1:20, "All the promises of God find their Yes in him" (ESV).

Old Covenant: God Found Fault (8:8)

> *God found fault with the people.* (HEBREWS 8:8)

We see that because the people could not perfectly obey the commands of the old covenant, God found fault with them. We keep wishing that God would grade on a curve—that he would take note of our sincerity and sacrifice. But he is an absolutely holy God, perfect in his justice. It takes only one sin to make us completely sinful. "Whoever keeps the whole law and yet stumbles at just one point is guilty of breaking all of it" (James 2:10).

New Covenant: God Forgives and Forgets (8:12)

> *I will forgive their wickedness and will remember their sins no more.* (HEBREWS 8:12)

In the new covenant, rather than simply finding fault, God offers forgiveness. And not only that, he says that he will "remember their sins no more" (8:12). So the first answer we find to the question "How will we get rid of our guilt?" is that we simply receive what is offered to us through the new covenant of grace given to us through Jesus. We simply open our hands and our hearts and receive the forgiveness that Jesus offers.

Receive Forgiveness

When God forgives, it doesn't mean he looks at our sin and says, "It doesn't matter. It is no big deal." When he said he would forgive our wickedness, he knew what it would cost. He knew that the price for forgiveness would be paid through the death of a perfect sacrifice—his own Son.

But this is *his* plan, *his* remedy for our problem of guilt. He has given the sacrifice so he can offer us his forgiveness, which it is up to us to receive.

Not only does he forgive us, he offers us the complete freedom of knowing that he will "remember [our] sins no more." This doesn't mean that our all-knowing God actually forgets what we've done. It means he no longer holds it against us. He recalls what we've done, but he will never throw our failure back in our faces. He doesn't treat us as our sins deserve. He treats us as if we had not sinned against him.

This is something for us to remember when other people hurt us and we think to ourselves, *Well, maybe I can forgive, but I can never forget!* We probably can't forget. We will probably always recall what they did or said that hurt us deeply. But as we become more like Christ, he gives us the grace to do what he does; he gives us the inner strength to refuse to hold those hurts against the people who have hurt us. We can actually treat them as though they'd never done it. That's how he treats us! This is a grace he provides to us so we can treat others the same way.

> When he said he would forgive our wickedness, he knew what it would cost. He knew that the price for forgiveness would be paid through the death of a perfect sacrifice—his own Son.

Old Covenant: God Turned Away (8:9)

We see in verse 9 that the sin of God's people caused him to turn away.

> *They did not remain faithful to my covenant, and I turned away from them, declares the Lord.* (HEBREWS 8:9)

Who can blame him? He had chosen the Israelites and delivered them and provided for them and loved them, and they complained and criticized and created a golden calf to bow down to. What they had done and who they had become were unacceptable. So God turned away.

But in the new covenant, God made a way to turn toward us, a way to make us acceptable. Not only that, he refuses to keep us at arm's distance. He makes us his own.

God is not looking for outward conformity. He wants internal transformation.

New Covenant: God Calls Us His Own (8:10)

Verse 10 shows how close God wants us to be.

I will be their God, and they will be my people. (HEBREWS 8:10)

My friend Jamie and her husband, Mark, just returned from China and brought home with them thirteen-month-old Glory (don't you just love that name!). For months they've had her picture, but Glory has been so far away. Because they loved her already, they did what was necessary to bring her home. They signed papers and paid money and bought diapers and made room in their home and in their hearts so that they could call Glory their own.

This is what God has done for you. In his grace, he offers you what you could never achieve on your own—acceptance. He makes you his own. However, the acceptance he offers is something you have to choose to receive.

Receive Acceptance

You might have heard someone teach that "God accepts you just the way you are." It isn't true. The truth is, we come to Jesus just as we are, with nothing to offer. But Jesus doesn't present us to his Father just as we are. He presents us in himself as *he* is. We hide ourselves in Jesus, and when we enter into God's presence, God sees Jesus instead of us.[19] This is what makes us acceptable to God.

Will you hide yourself in Jesus and receive this gift of acceptance by God?

Old Covenant: Laws Chiseled in Stone

The old covenant was delivered when the finger of God wrote the Ten Commandments on tablets of stone. And God instructed the Israelites to write his law on their foreheads and put it on their doorposts and teach it to their children. But it was all on the outside. It was on the tablets and on their walls, but not in their hearts. They knew what God wanted, but they didn't have the will or the power to obey. They didn't have the want-to.

God is not looking for outward conformity. He wants internal transformation. Remember that Jesus was offended by the rigid religious rituals of the

Pharisees, who went through the motions of obeying the Law but whose hearts were far from God. He called them whitewashed tombs, full of deadness on the inside.

He wants us to be alive on the inside—alive to him, alive to his ways, alive to his Word, alive with the joy of knowing him, alive with desire to please him. So rather than merely providing us with a law of outward conformity, he gets to the heart of the matter.

New Covenant: Law Carved on Our Hearts (8:10)

> *I will put my laws in their minds and write them on their hearts.*
> (HEBREWS 8:10)

In the new covenant God provides for our need for holiness by putting his law in our minds and on our hearts. In this way, he gives us the want-to. His Holy Spirit indwelling us moves us from following a list of rules into a loving relationship. We find that as we enjoy him, as we delight ourselves in him, he gives us the desires of our hearts. And because he has written his law on our hearts, when we are given the desires of our hearts, we find that what we want most is to please him.

Are you so weighed down by guilt that your desire for doing what is pleasing to God has been dampened? Will you open your heart to him and fill your mind with his Word so that he can carve what is pleasing to him into your heart? Will you open your heart to receive the desire to please him?

And because he has written his law on our hearts, when we are given the desires of our hearts, we find that what we want most is to please him.

Receive Desire

You cannot work up the desire to please God on your own. You must receive this desire as a gift of his grace in your life. Ask for it. Cultivate it. Receive it.

Isn't it interesting that the way we get rid of guilt in God's economy is not to "do" but to "receive"? We do not have to purge our guilt by inflicting pain on ourselves or by giving a million dollars to charity or by signing up to work in a soup kitchen this Thanksgiving. This is what makes the new covenant better than the old covenant. The old covenant of the Law required perfect obedience but offered no power to obey.

The new covenant is a gift of grace. The new covenant requires only that we humble ourselves enough to confess our sins and receive God's forgiveness, that we offer ourselves to him and receive his acceptance, and that we open ourselves to him and receive a desire for holiness written onto our hearts by God himself.

A BETTER SACRIFICE

If we're honest, most of us would just rather not talk about all this blood sacrifice stuff. It seems a little primitive. It is very messy and unsightly. And really, we want to say to God, why all the blood? Why is it that you demand a blood sacrifice for sin? Isn't there some other way?

After all, we live in a society where people applaud when they read, "No animals were harmed in the making of this film." We buy boneless, skinless chicken breasts wrapped in plastic. If you're like me, the closest you come to dealing with the carcass of a dead animal is after Thanksgiving dinner. How can our modern minds accept and understand the sacrificial slaughter of thousands of animals—let alone the human sacrifice of Jesus?

> I can't help but wonder if we would take sin as lightly as we do today if we had to regularly slit the throat of an animal to seek atonement for it.

We could estimate that there were more than a million animals sacrificed during the thousand-plus years of the old covenant. So considering that each bull's sacrifice spilled a gallon or two of blood, and each goat's, a quart, it is mind boggling to think of all that blood and all those burning carcasses.[20] The old covenant rested on a sea of spilled blood. In fact, there was so much blood, an entire Temple irrigation system had to be created for it.[21]

All the blood served as an unavoidable megaphone that shouted about the seriousness of sin, reminding the people that sin both brings and demands death. The blood was like a neon sign in the window of their minds that was constantly flashing: Sin brings death . . . sin brings death . . . sin brings death.

The blood helped the Israelites see the seriousness of sin. And I can't help but wonder if we would take sin as lightly as we do today if we had to regularly slit the throat of an animal to seek atonement for it.

Old Sacrifices: The Blood of Animals Covered Up Sin (9:9-10)

> *This is an illustration for the present time, indicating that the gifts and sacrifices being offered were not able to clear the conscience of the worshiper. They are only a matter of food and drink and various ceremonial washings—external regulations applying until the time of the new order.*
> (HEBREWS 9:9-10)

We tend to think of the Old Testament sacrifices as being payment for sin or the process necessary to obtain forgiveness for sin. That's the way I've always understood it. But in reality, the sacrifices were not a means for obtaining forgiveness or salvation. Obedience in offering the sacrifices as God prescribed was an act of faith, offered believing that God would do what is necessary to provide cleansing and forgiveness. But the sacrifices themselves didn't do the job. They were merely a superficial solution.

King David evidently understood this. Agonizing with guilt over his sin, he wrote, "You do not delight in sacrifice, or I would bring it; you do not take pleasure in burnt offerings" (Psalm 51:16).

The blood of animals didn't take sin away; it just covered sin up, like my sweater covers up the spot on my blouse. The priest sprinkled the blood on the mercy seat in an effort to cover up the sin. But it wasn't taken away. And since the blood didn't remove the sin, it didn't do away with the guilt.

In fact, there were only certain types of sins the sacrifices covered. Hebrews 9:7 says that the sacrifices only covered sins of ignorance—sins that were committed unintentionally, unknowingly, but were nonetheless offensive to God. There was no provision in the old covenant's sacrificial system for forgiveness for premeditated, willful sins. The ones who sinned on purpose found no remedy for their guilt in the sacrificial system.[22] This is why we needed a better sacrifice, a perfect sacrifice.

New Sacrifice: The Blood of Christ Cleaned Up Sin (9:14)

So what is the remedy for our guilty conscience? The blood of Jesus.

> *The blood of Christ, who through the eternal Spirit offered himself unblemished to God, [will] cleanse our consciences from acts that lead to death, so that we may serve the living God!* (HEBREWS 9:14)

I know it sounds archaic and perhaps even ridiculous. Here we are living in a modern age with cell phones and space travel and bone-marrow transplants, but our problem is fundamentally the same as it has always been—consciences that need to be cleansed. Our consciences condemn us and make us feel unacceptable to God.[23] We're alienated from him because we know we're not good enough to come to him. And the answer is as ancient as the old rugged cross.

Talking about the blood of Jesus may seem primitive or old-fashioned or unappealing to you. But if you have a conscience that needs to be cleansed, the blood of Christ is precious to you. It is your only hope for the inner cleansing you crave.

The blood of Christ has the power not just to cover over our sin but also to cleanse us of sin so that we can draw near to a holy God. The point isn't to make us look good on the outside. The blood of Christ is the only cleansing agent in the universe that can cleanse us on the inside, where our consciences condemn us.

If you have a conscience that needs to be cleansed, the blood of Christ is precious to you. It is your only hope for the inner cleansing you crave.

Have Your Conscience Cleansed

The only way we get rid of our guilt is to have our consciences cleansed. The blood of Christ takes away our need to keep covering up the spots and stains sin has left behind on our hearts and in our minds. Our sin is removed, so we are no longer enslaved by the guilt sin brings. The cleansing power of Christ's blood sets us free.

What have you done that racks you with the kind of guilt that eats away at your joy, erodes your relationships, and keeps you from moving closer to God? Can you see that with his own blood, Jesus has written in large red letters across your life, "Forgiven! Clean! Mine!"?

Can you see that with his own blood, Jesus has written in large red letters across your life, "Forgiven! Clean! Mine!"?

Old Sacrifices: Repeated Endlessly to Remind Us of Sin (10:3)

Not only was the old system of sacrifices unable to remove sin, the repetitive nature of the sacrifices spoke to the reality that we can never escape sin. The covering of animal blood for sin lasted only until the next sin. There was no escaping the constant reminder of sin and the heavy load of constant guilt.

> *Those sacrifices are an annual reminder of sins.*
> (HEBREWS 10:3)

That was what the sacrifices were meant to do—remind us of sin. But they couldn't free us of sin.

The blood of the sacrifices was like a bottle of medicine that a person with a chronic illness takes every day. She takes the medicine to get some relief from the symptoms, but the root cause—the root illness—does not go away; it is not cured. This is what the sacrifices did. And so every time they looked at the medicine bottle—the blood of the animal sacrifice—it served as a reminder of the medicine's ineffectiveness to take care of the root problem. It was a reminder that they were still sick with sin and that the sacrifice was only a temporary fix.[24]

Tomorrow's sins would demand tomorrow's sacrifice, and on and on it would go, never offering any full relief. A constant reminder. The annual repetition of the ceremony was evidence that the previous year's sacrifices had not done the job. Another year, another lamb, another sacrifice, and the sin was still there.

It all spoke to the need for a perfect sacrifice, the ultimate sacrifice that would finally be good enough, vast enough, to end those treks to the Temple and satisfy once and for all the righteous demands of a just and holy God.

New Sacrifice: Once for All to Free Us from Sin (9:26-28)

> *Then Christ would have had to suffer many times since the creation of the world. But now he has appeared once for all at the end of the ages to*

> *do away with sin by the sacrifice of himself. Just as man is destined to die once, and after that to face judgment, so Christ was sacrificed once to take away the sins of many people; and he will appear a second time, not to bear sin, but to bring salvation to those who are waiting for him.* (HEBREWS 9:26-28)

Verse 26 describes the sacrifice of Jesus at the "consummation" or the "end of the ages." When the final, perfect, sufficient sacrifice was slain, it was the climax of history. The death of Jesus was not just one event in a line of similar historical events. It was the most significant, supreme event of all time.[25] It was the sacrifice of the most valuable person in the universe. And it finally brought an end to the need for Temple sacrifices.

It was enough. Jesus was enough. His sacrifice took care of our sin problem once and for all. The sacrifice of Jesus finally set us free from debilitating guilt.

Stop Punishing Yourself

I have a friend who wanted to wait until she was married to have sex. But in her senior year of college she found herself pregnant. Wanting to erase the mistake and move on with her life, she had an abortion and promised herself she would not have sex again until she was married. But only two years later she was pregnant again, and once again she chose to abort the baby. Eventually she married and started a family, but she couldn't shake the guilt from her self-centered choices, and for years she was miserable. She believed that God forgave her, but she could not accept that she was forgiven. The guilt consumed her.

> Why should you listen to Satan bringing up your past to accuse you if God does not do so?

One day her sister-in-law suggested that the voice inside her head and her heart that was constantly condemning her and keeping her racked with guilt was not God's voice but Satan's. She suggested it was Satan who wanted to keep my friend stewing in her sin rather than enjoying the freedom of God's forgiveness.

Remember that when God forgives us, he promises that he will never again remember our sins; he chooses not to bring up our sin or hold it against us. But Satan the accuser brings it back to rub our noses in it and make us feel guilty. Why should you listen to Satan bringing up your past to accuse you if God does not do so?

The only way to cleanse a guilty conscience is to embrace the absolute and all-encompassing forgiveness of God. Only then can we make a fresh start. Nothing we try on our own can assuage our guilt—not the mind games to justify our actions, not the escape mechanisms to numb our feelings, not the religious performances to prove ourselves worthy.

If God says we are forgiven, who are we to keep punishing ourselves? If we keep believing we deserve to be punished, it's as if we are saying that we are greater than God, that our judgment is higher than his.

Can you see that the magnificent sacrifice of Jesus is big enough—costly enough—to cover whatever you've done that has thrown you into a prison of self-punishment? Won't you choose to stop punishing yourself and place your faith in his once-for-all sacrifice for sin?

Can you see that the magnificent sacrifice of Jesus is big enough–costly enough–to cover whatever you've done that has thrown you into a prison of self-punishment?

Old Sacrifices: No Progress toward Holiness (10:11)

In chapter 10 of Hebrews, we find one more way we shed the guilt that keeps us bound up, one more way that the sacrifice of Jesus provides what we need to get rid of our guilt. It's the secret to standing before God with confidence. But first we must see the contrasting weakness of the old sacrificial system in verses 1-4:

> *The law is only a shadow of the good things that are coming—not the realities themselves. For this reason it can never, by the same sacrifices repeated endlessly year after year, make perfect those who draw near to worship. If it could, would they not have stopped being offered? For the worshipers would have been cleansed once for all, and would no longer have felt guilty for their sins. But those sacrifices are an annual reminder of sins, because it is impossible for the blood of bulls and goats to take away sins.*

The weakness of the old sacrificial system was that it had to be repeated day after day, year after year, never helping the worshipper, make any progress toward holiness. Verse 1 says it could "never . . . make perfect those who draw near to worship," and verse 11 says that the sacrifices can "never take away sins."

New Sacrifice: Once for All (10:14)

But in verse 14 we see how the sacrifice of Jesus is dramatically different:

> *By one sacrifice he has made perfect forever those who are being made holy.*
> (HEBREWS 10:14)

Unlike the repeated Old Testament sacrifices that covered sin, the one-time sacrifice of Jesus removed all sin—past and present—providing a clean slate to sinners.

Notice when these things happened. He "*has made* perfect"—something that's already been done. Those who "*are being made* holy"—something that's happening right now. The perfection has been accomplished in the past. The process of being made holy is continual.

So in what way are we perfected? Our slates have been wiped clean. We've been completely forgiven. Our debts have been paid. Because we are in Christ, we stand before God perfected. When he looks at us, he doesn't count our sins against us. We are covered, not in the spots and stains left behind by our failures and mistakes, but in the robes of righteousness given to us by Christ. He has given us his own righteousness in place of our sin-spotted rags.

So if we're perfect, why do we need to continue to be made holy? Because while our standing before God is perfected, we all know that is not the reality in our lives.

Think of it this way. When a person is judged "not guilty" in court, does it mean that person is innocent? Not necessarily (think O. J. Simpson). It is the same for us. We are judged "not guilty," not because we are innocent, but because the blood of Jesus has washed away our guilt and covered us in the innocence of Christ.

But in practical terms, we're still sinners. We still sin.

So what does it mean that we are "being made holy"? It means that we are becoming closer and closer in reality to what we've been declared to be in the courtroom of heaven. Being sanctified means that the gap is being closed between what we've been declared to be in Christ and who we are in our flesh.

Experience Ever-Increasing Holiness

Do you find in your life a growing hunger for holiness and a growing distaste for this world? God is setting you apart for himself. Two thousand years ago he accomplished your perfection through his sacrifice on the cross. And now he lives inside you, equipping you with the power you need to live differently from the rest of the world, the power to change, the power to become more like Jesus.

Remember that song by Paul Simon "Fifty Ways to Leave Your Lover"? Well, there are at least fifteen ways people try to get rid of their guilt. Some of them will likely sound very familiar to you.

1. Deny their sin.
2. Excuse their sin.
3. Redefine sin.
4. Run from their sin.
5. Ignore their sin.
6. Pretend they have not sinned.
7. Lie about their sin.
8. Cover up their sin.
9. Justify their sin.
10. Blame others for their sin.
11. Drown their sin.
12. Look for ways and people who will make them feel comfortable with their sin.
13. Try to pay for their sin.
14. Destroy their conscience.
15. Try various forms of religion.[26]

But there is only one way to experience pervasive, permanent cleansing from all the rebellion and regrets of your past: to lay your guilt before God and let him wash it away with the blood of his Son. God does not demand your blood to cover your sin. He offers you his own.

Jesus provides the remedy for all of our rebellion and regrets. Won't you come to Jesus and let him get rid of your guilt?

Jesus provides the remedy for all of our rebellion and regrets.

CHAPTER 7

why should you keep on believing?

HEBREWS 10:19-39

I READ TODAY THAT two weeks ago in China, police arrested fifty key leaders of underground churches. These church leaders had organized a retreat to discuss how best to help the poor, the orphaned, and migrant urban populations. The news account I read says that "some were beaten and interrogated while in custody." It goes on to say:

> Many of the leaders taken into custody saw the event as an open door to share the Word of God. Pastor Zhang Mingxuan, the first Chinese to have the title "evangelist" printed on a business card, preached the gospel to interrogators. At the end of the questioning, one of Zhang's exhausted interrogators was quoted telling him, "Man, you preach too hard!"

> One church leader, 35-year-old law school graduate Ms. Dai Hong, was taken to a room on the second floor and beaten by two male policemen because she demanded that they show her their identification before divulging hers.
>
> Nearly 60 Religious Affairs Bureau officials, along with their hired local guards and 30 police vehicles, reluctantly and shamefully left the scene after releasing the pastors. The bold Christian witnesses joyfully said farewell to the guards with songs of praise and worship to the Lord![27]

Today there are many believers around the world who face the same reality of growing persecution that the people who originally received the letter to the Hebrews faced. It wasn't easy for these early Christians to be followers of Christ. Followers of Christ experienced having their property confiscated, being stoned to death, being ostracized in the business and trading community, being rejected by their families in a culture where families were everything, and losing their welcome at the Temple, which was a central point of Jewish life.

Evidently the group of Hebrews the letter was written to had not yet faced death, even though they experienced significant persecution. Hebrews 12:4 says, "You have not yet resisted to the point of shedding your blood." But we read in Hebrews 10:33-34 that they were "publicly exposed to insult and persecution" and that they "joyfully accepted the confiscation of [their] property."

This kind of persecution caused many to think about giving up this new Jesus-centered way of life. Nagging doubts about whether or not Jesus had to take the place of Judaism were creeping in, which made perseverance all the more difficult. Many were tempted to turn back to the safety of Judaism as the cost for following Christ began to escalate.

Such persecution truly seems on the other side of the world or in another era to those of us living in the freedom of the West, doesn't it? And even though we experience the occasional ridiculing comment by someone who sees Christianity as small minded or backward, we really don't have much experience with significant challenges to our faith—the kind of challenges that force us to count the cost.

But what will happen when and if, one day, it becomes inconvenient—even dangerous—to identify ourselves as Christians and meet with other Christians? Will we be able to sing so easily what I sang on a recent Sunday morning at my church—words sung by Christians for centuries? These words are perhaps so familiar to us that we hardly realize what we're saying when we sing "A Mighty Fortress Is Our God":

Let goods and kindred go,
This mortal life also
The body they may kill;
God's truth abideth still

When we face problems, and as we prepare for persecution that may be ahead, we need to ask ourselves, Why should I keep on believing even when it may cost me what I don't want to pay? And what does faith look like in the face of problems and persecution?

To those Hebrews whose faith began to waver as they began to suffer, to those thousands of Christians around the world today who put their lives on the line on a daily basis out of love for Jesus, and to those of us who deep inside are struggling with questions about whether or not the life of faith is what we thought it would be, this writer says, Don't give up. Don't stop. Don't waver. Keep going.

PERSEVERE BY . . . DRAWING NEAR TO GOD

Let us draw near to God. (HEBREWS 10:22)

The essence of perseverance is a continued journey toward God, an increasingly intimate relationship with God.

The essence of perseverance is a continued journey toward God, an increasingly intimate relationship with God.

Do you ever look at someone else and envy her walk with God and wonder what her secret is? There is no secret formula for an intimate relationship with God—just as there are no secret formulas for making human relationships work. But there are conditions. In verse 22 we discover three conditions to drawing near to Christ in the intimate relationship that we crave.

> *Let us draw near to God with a sincere heart in full assurance of faith, having our hearts sprinkled to cleanse us from a guilty conscience and having our bodies washed with pure water.* (HEBREWS 10:22)

First, to draw near to God we need a sincere heart. A sincere heart is one that is devoid of hypocrisy. No mixed motives or divided loyalties, only devotion.

Someone with a heart devoid of hypocrisy does not pray dramatically for show while rarely making time for personal prayer. Someone with a sincere heart does not come to God looking only for what she can get. A person with a heart that is completely devoted eliminates many "good" things from her schedule and her life so she can give her first love quality time and attention. If we want to draw near, we can't let other loves steal our hearts from our first love, and we can't make our relationship with God about putting on a show for others or about getting what God's got. We draw near because we want God himself—sincerely.

Second, drawing near to God requires a sincere heart in full assurance of faith. There's no hesitation, only trust. If we want to draw near to God, we can't keep waiting for a better time, a better teacher, a better church, a better book, a better anything.

Don't wait. You don't know what is around the corner. Draw near to God with no hesitation and no holding back. You'll have to stop hesitating and worrying and obsessing, and simply choose to trust God. You'll find yourself walking closer and closer to him as, with each step and every surrender, he proves himself trustworthy.

Third, we need to have our hearts "sprinkled to cleanse us from a guilty conscience" and "our bodies washed with pure water" (10:22). No guilt, only purity.

This is a reference to what we looked at in the last chapter—that under the old covenant the people were sprinkled with the blood of animals to symbolize cleansing, but the cleansing was never complete. In this new covenant, the completely adequate blood of Christ cleanses us on the inside. Rather than being cleansed like the priests were through continually washing themselves with basins of sacred water, we are purified as the Word of God washes over our lives.

Drawing near—and continuing to draw near—is what this passage, and the whole book of Hebrews, encourages us to do. But this doesn't just happen. Drawing near requires a focused, single-hearted effort.

What do you need to drop from your schedule so that you can draw near? What relationship do you need to withdraw from so you can draw near? What doubt do you need to deal with so you can draw near? What sin or failure do you need to see as washed away so you can draw near?

PERSEVERE BY . . . HOLDING ON TO HOPE

> *Let us hold unswervingly to the hope we profess, for he who promised is faithful.* (HEBREWS 10:23)

The hope these early Christians professed was salvation solely through the sacrifice of Jesus. The author was saying, "Don't waver on the source and surety of your salvation." There is encouragement here to keep holding on and standing firm.

No wavering, only steadfastness.

Several years ago we had a big pear tree crack and fall over in our backyard. We had three evergreen trees planted in its place, but one of them just would not stand up. The slightest breeze would blow it down. So one time when my parents visited and were looking for fix-it projects at our house, my dad found an old broom handle in the garage and stuck it deep into the ground and tied the always-falling-down tree to it. That way, no matter how much the wind blew, the tree didn't fall down again. It has flourished and grown and is still holding steady.

When you choose to hold on to the hope of your salvation—Jesus himself—it is as if you drive a stake into the ground and hold on for dear life, so that when the winds of adversity or persecution come your way, you can hold steady without falling. You can persevere.

The key to holding steady has everything to do with the ground the stake is driven into. If we drive it into sand, it won't hold. The ground must be solid.

What solid ground are we going to drive our stake into to hold on to hope? Verse 23 says, "He who promised is

> If you want to hold on to hope, you will have to choose to place all your confidence in what God has promised—and then keep holding on.

faithful." The soil we're digging into is the very Word of God—wholly reliable and true. The stake of our hope is dug deep into the soil of God's promise to save completely. Jesus' statement that "God did not send his Son into the world to condemn the world, but to save the world through him" (John 3:17) is the solid ground into which you can drive the stake of your life.

You are only foolish to keep holding on to hope if the foundation of your hope is insecure. Our foundation for hope is God's Word and his promises. If you want to hold on to hope, you will have to choose to place all your confidence in what God has promised—and then keep holding on.

A PROFILE OF HOLDING ON TO HOPE

Holding on to hope is exactly what my friend Michelle Alm is doing. A while back I received this e-mail from her:

> Dear Nancy,
>
> Early in the morning on Saturday, October 9, my son, Vince, was in a serious car accident. As a result of his injuries, he is a C6 quadriplegic. This tragedy has rocked my world in a way I did not even know was possible. I am very thankful that you have gone ahead of me in sadness. Seeing that you survived it is the hope I need to move ahead.

> Dear Michelle,
>
> The words "he is a C6 quadriplegic" don't seem to do justice to the immensity of this trauma. I can't imagine how hard this has been and how hard the future must look for you and for Vince. I went for a walk after I got your e-mail to talk to God. Sometimes I have to check in with him to make sure it is all still true—his goodness, his sovereignty, his purpose in suffering, his desire for our ultimate good, his love, heaven. Because if it isn't true, we are completely without hope in this life, and it is all meaningless. If it isn't true, then pointing hurting people toward him is actually very cruel. But if it is

> true, then we can trust him; we can love him, no matter what happens. And I firmly believe it is true; he is true! In these days, as your world has been rocked so significantly, grab on to what is true and determine to hold on to it even as the winds of doubt and despair blow over you. It is not necessarily great faith or great courage that will get you through this (although that is what others no doubt will see). It is holding on to what you know is true about God and refusing to let go.
>
> About a year later, after taking a sabbatical from her job to care for Vince, she sent me this e-mail, a testimony of perseverance:
>
> The return to work has been an amazing opportunity to be more than I ever wanted to be. My much-loved position was filled by someone else in my absence. Though my compensation has remained the same, the quality of my days has been substantially affected. This has brought with it a daily opportunity to trust and treasure God unconditionally at a level I never imagined possible. To count it all joy when the joy is so deeply hidden may be the greatest challenge of all. This in conjunction with my home life changes has led to a level of disappointment that compares to nothing I have ever known. The question I often ask myself is if I can trust and treasure God even when not one single thing goes my way. Most days the answer is yes, which can only be attributed to God's amazing grace. On the days when the burden of the sadness takes me over and discouragement wins, I, like you, check in to make sure it is still true—his goodness, his sovereignty, his purpose in suffering, his desire for our ultimate good, his love, heaven. To have Jesus . . . nothing compares.

You can hold on, because he who promised is faithful. Not sometimes faithful, sometimes true. Always, infinitely reliable and true. When you know you can trust what God has said, you will be able to hold on to hope. You will be able to persevere.

PERSEVERE BY . . . ENCOURAGING EACH OTHER

> *Let us consider how we may spur one another on toward love and good deeds.* (HEBREWS 10:24)

Notice that verse 24 says we need to "consider" how to spur one another on to love and good deeds. Here we see that encouraging others well requires that we think about it and work at it. For some of us, this doesn't come naturally. But our goal is to live a life of love that encourages others to love well too.

As we consider how to spur one another on to love and good deeds, our first idea might be to tell other people what to do. But the truth is, the most effective way of spurring someone else to love others well is to love others well ourselves. No talk without the walk.

A while ago, Matt and I stopped at the grocery store for a few items. There was a well-dressed man who exited the store shortly before we did. Coming toward us in the parking lot was a woman who was probably in her late sixties, holding the hand of a girl about ten or twelve years old who had an unusual-shaped body and facial characteristics reflecting a genetic anomaly. They were both wearing worn-out coats, and they were holding hands as they walked toward the store.

I saw the man stop the woman and the girl and hand them something and say, "God bless you," as he walked away. It took me a minute to realize that he had handed them some cash. I don't think they asked for it. I think he just saw their need and stepped out of his comfort zone to meet it.

Observing this moved me. I determined that the next time I saw an opportunity like that, I would take action myself. I imagined how good he was feeling as he drove away. And I was thinking how that simple action might have impacted Matt if I had given the woman some of our hard-earned money.

Without even knowing it, without saying a word to me, this man spurred me on to love and good works.

Consider how you might do that for those who are watching you. For your spouse who is watching. For your kids who are watching. For your neighbors who are watching. For fellow motorists who are watching. Not because you want to impress anyone or because you're trying to earn your way into God's favor, but because you recognize that what you do to please God can inspire someone else to want to please him too. Simply love others well, and thereby spur others on to love well too.

> *Let us not give up meeting together, as some are in the habit of doing, but let us encourage one another—and all the more as you see the Day approaching.* (Hebrews 10:25)

The more persecution increased, the more these believers were tempted to stop meeting and worshipping together. They were deserting the body of Christ as the cost of being associated with those who followed Christ became greater. These struggling, persecuted believers needed the encouragement of being with other Christians and enjoying Christ together. It would give them the courage to keep going, the confidence to know that they were not alone.

Christianity is corporate. There are no lone rangers in the body. We need each other. And we need to encourage each other. Maybe you are full of courage today. If so, then offer some of yours to someone else. Don't operate in the body looking only to get your needs met. Look for needs that you can uniquely meet, and in the process you'll find your needs uniquely met.

Don't operate in the body looking only to get your needs met. Look for needs that you can uniquely meet, and in the process you'll find your needs uniquely met.

The truth is, it is not the fear of persecution that causes most of us to forsake the body of Christ. We forsake the body when someone criticizes us, when someone hurts our feelings, when someone refuses to do things our way. The body of Christ is made up of needy, imperfect people, some of whom just rub us the wrong way. But if we want to love others well, we will have to stop competing and stop criticizing and start encouraging.

Who needs a word of encouragement today that you could uniquely give—that would mean something special because it came from you? Persevere in encouraging others, even when—and perhaps especially when—you wish someone would encourage you.

PERSEVERE BECAUSE . . . REJECTING CHRIST RESULTS IN JUDGMENT

Having seen what perseverance looks like, we now see in the next several verses the negative motivation we need to keep persevering.

Judgment for sin is certain. And judgment for sin will be terrifying for those who are not protected from it.

This passage introduces one of the most politically incorrect words in the English language today: judgment. In our postmodern culture's mind-set, the ultimate abomination is to pass judgment on another person. And to say that God will judge sin is considered an old-fashioned, out-of-date scare tactic.

But if we are going to base what we believe on what the Bible teaches and not on how we think things ought to work, then we have to affirm that judgment for sin is certain. And judgment for sin will be terrifying for those who are not protected from it.

We like to categorize sins as little sins and big sins. We put murder and adultery and the like way up at the top of the list. And while all sins are serious affronts to God, it makes sense that if Jesus said the *greatest commandment* is to "love the Lord your God with all your heart and with all your soul and with all your mind" (Matthew 22:37), then the greatest sin must be to refuse to love God at all—to refuse to respond to the love he holds out to us.

How does a person reject Christ? One way we reject Christ and his sacrifice for sin is by our refusal to let go of sin.

> *If we deliberately keep on sinning after we have received the knowledge of the truth, no sacrifice for sins is left, but only a fearful expectation of judgment and of raging fire that will consume the enemies of God.*
> (HEBREWS 10:26-27)

Am I suggesting that as Christians we will never sin? Of course not! What I'm saying is that people who say, "I know it is sin but I am going to do it anyway" and keep doing it are basically rejecting the sacrifice of Christ. They are saying,

"I don't need you or your holiness. I want to live my way, not your way." Such people are, in effect, rejecting Christ.

I can't help but think of an elder in a church who left his wife and children for another woman. The pastor and the other elders confronted him with his sin, and his response was, "God will forgive me." His pastor told him, "I'm not so sure." The problem was not the scope of God's forgiveness but the man's rejection of Christ's holiness—evidenced by his refusal to relinquish known sin.

When we deliberately keep sinning after receiving the knowledge of the truth, with no sense of conviction or desire to change, this passage tells us "no sacrifice for sins is left, but only a fearful expectation of judgment" (10:26-27).

If we keep deliberately sinning, it is as if we see Christ on the cross and just walk right over him.

Yes, grace does abound. But when we know and have experienced the truth of the gospel, and when we choose to keep walking in deliberate sin away from God, we are, in effect, rejecting Christ and his sacrifice for sin. A bold rejection of the holiness of Christ calls into question the genuineness of our saving connection to him.

There is a phrase in verse 29 that almost brings me to tears: "Do you think a man deserves to be punished who has trampled the Son of God under foot, who has treated as an unholy thing the blood of the covenant that sanctified him?"

Imagine trampling the Son of God underfoot.

When you walk along a sidewalk and you look down and spot a dollar, you see it as something of value. So you don't walk on by or step on it, you pick it up. But when you see a discarded gum wrapper or a ticket stub, you just walk over it because it is worthless.

In the same way, if we keep deliberately sinning, it is as if we see Christ on the cross and just walk right over him, "trample him under foot," because we see him as worthless. When we do this, we have "insulted the Spirit" (10:29).

Don't fool yourself into thinking that you can keep walking toward sin, trampling underfoot the Son of God, and that God owes you and will save you from judgment because you prayed a prayer or walked down an aisle one day. Let me repeat. As a believer you will sin. Rejecting God is not about the sin you repeatedly struggle against. It's about a heart attitude and mind-set toward sin in which there is no struggle. You just give yourself to it, choosing the temporal pleasure of sin over the eternal promises of God.

If you find that you sin repeatedly and deliberately with no sense of conviction or sadness over your sin, then you need to question if you have really placed your faith in Christ. Your choices are saying to Jesus, "I don't need you or your holiness!" Your casual approach to sin has, as verse 29 says, "insulted the Spirit of grace."

If you choose to rebel and reject Christ, you are choosing to incur God's wrath, and you will be judged. As it says in verse 31, "It is a dreadful thing to fall into the hands of the living God." This is not manipulation or a scare tactic. This is the truth.

PERSEVERE BECAUSE . . . YOU WILL BE REWARDED

In the previous section of chapter 10, the author has given us the negative motivation we need to persevere. In the rest of chapter 10, he motivates us in another way—by drawing a picture that is a complete contrast to the person who has rejected Christ.

> *Remember those earlier days after you had received the light, when you stood your ground in a great contest in the face of suffering. Sometimes you were publicly exposed to insult and persecution; at other times you stood side by side with those who were so treated. You sympathized with those in prison and joyfully accepted the confiscation of your property, because you knew that you yourselves had better and lasting possessions. So do not throw away your confidence; it will be richly rewarded. You need to persevere so that when you have done the will of God, you will receive what he has promised.* (HEBREWS 10:32-36)

Here the author is cheering on those who have made the choice to persevere in the face of suffering and persecution. He recounts their faithfulness to stand side by side with those who were facing persecution and imprisonment. This writer says to the Hebrews and to us:

Stand your ground in the face of suffering.

Stand strong in the face of persecution.

Stand side by side with those who are being persecuted.

As he describes these faithful believers who suffered and were persecuted, he says they "joyfully accepted the confiscation of [their] property" (10:34).

Joyfully? Hello!? We get a little annoyed when our next-door neighbors repeatedly mow a little too far into our property as if they think it is theirs! We don't want anyone taking what is ours. And we read that these people "joyfully accepted" having what was theirs taken from them? They patiently endured significant suffering and persecution and stood with others at great risk and cost to themselves and to their families? How could they do that?

They were able to let go of things here because they knew they had "better and lasting" possessions waiting for them in heaven. They believed their perseverance would be rewarded with something better.

These people took Jesus at his word when he said, "Do not store up for yourselves treasures on earth, where moth and rust destroy, and where thieves break in and steal. But store up for yourselves treasures in heaven, where moth and rust do not destroy, and where thieves do not break in and steal. For where your treasure is, there your heart will be also" (Matthew 6:19-21). That was the secret to their joy.

They were able to let go of things here because they knew they had "better and lasting" possessions waiting for them in heaven. They believed their perseverance would be rewarded with something better.

The writer of Hebrews reminds his readers of the "earlier days after you had received the light, when you stood your ground in a great contest in the face of suffering" (10:32). He affirms their past faith and confidence, which gave them the courage they needed to stand their ground and stand strong when their suffering seemed unbearable and when the pressures of persecution seemed overwhelming. He reminds them of their sacrificial obedience in standing side by side with others who were persecuted for their faith.

And he tells them that all their sacrifice and suffering will be worth it—that what they let go of here will be returned to them with interest later.

In fact, he tells them that they will be "richly rewarded" (10:35). No skimping. No disappointment. They will receive what God has promised, and it will be more than they could ever dream. The reward God promises them for their patient perseverance in suffering and persecution—and the reward God has promised you—is really coming. It is not a pie-in-the-sky hope. It is a reality not yet realized.

The reward God promises them for their patient perseverance in suffering and persecution—and the reward God has promised you—is really coming. It is not a pie-in-the-sky hope. It is a reality not yet realized.

What have you given up out of love for Christ? Have you traded leisure or acceptance or comfort for serving Christ, being rejected for upholding the gospel, being disrespected for obeying God?

This writer says to us, Stand your ground in the face of suffering. You can do it. Stand strong in the face of persecution. Keep it up. Stand side by side with those who are being persecuted. Have courage. Keep going.

And he offers us this assurance: It will be worth it! It will be worth everything that it has cost you and will cost you as you continue to persevere.

You will be richly rewarded! You will receive what God has promised!

PERSEVERE BECAUSE . . . YOU ARE ONE WHO LIVES BY FAITH

"My righteous one will live by faith. And if he shrinks back, I will not be pleased with him." But we are not of those who shrink back and are destroyed, but of those who believe and are saved. (HEBREWS 10:38-39)

When I am being introduced to someone while I'm with my parents, they love to put me next to my mother and say something like, "Can you tell whose daughter she is?" In fact, for my birthday this year, my mother gave me a little stuffed bear looking into a mirror that says, "Mirror, mirror on the wall, I've become my mother after all!"

Some days I look in the mirror and realize it is true! I am becoming my mother. If you look at me and then at my mother, you know instantly whose child I am.

And while we're on the topic, you might as well know what I inherited from my father. My maiden name is Jinks. Nancy Jinks. After years of being teased about my name, I didn't mind trading it in for Guthrie. Besides, there are some qualities Jinkses are known for that I haven't always appreciated. Jinkses can be loud and opinionated, so I find myself trying to be quiet and soft spoken to be in dramatic contrast. But Jinkses are also generous and look for practical ways to help people in times of need. Jinkses love the church and love God's people. Jinkses live life to the fullest.

So I suppose, when I walk into a room looking every bit like my mother, my voice carrying above the crowd, or when I offer you a bed to sleep in or come to see you when you are in the hospital, it is a reflection of the family I come from.

In this passage, the writer to the Hebrews is appealing to the "family traits" of the people of faith. Living by faith and persevering are what we do. We are not people who shrink back in the face of persecution. We are people who believe and keep on believing.

When you choose to live by faith and keep believing in the face of opposition, people can see the family resemblance. They recognize whose you are.

They also see what you believe. And it is the power of what you believe that will enable you to persevere when the going gets tough. What you know to be true—because it is what God has said—will become the foundation of the decisions you make and the actions you take. Your perseverance reflects what you believe—that what God has said is trustworthy and true, that his promises of salvation are reliable.

That promise of salvation is the foundation and destination that keeps us living by faith. And so, based on what God has said, we can trust his promise that perseverance is the pathway that leads us to salvation. Salvation from judgment. Salvation to eternal life in the presence of God. That's what you're going for, right? Then keep going.

Do you sometimes wonder if this walk of faith will be worth it? At times are you tempted to say, "I was looking for a Christianity in which God answers all my prayers the way I want him to, I don't have any problems, and life becomes simpler and easier"? Salvation was "sold" to some of us as something it's not, and we were mistakenly convinced that it would solve all our problems in this life. So when we run into prayers that are not answered the way we wanted or problems that don't get fixed on our timetable or troubles that we thought God would protect us from, we have second thoughts about what we've bought into. Having come to Christ with a consumer mentality, we're tempted to take our lives back into our own hands, to turn away from following Christ when we discover he is leading us toward the Cross.

Will you determine to keep on believing, no matter what?

I talk to and correspond with many people who are facing sorrow and difficulty—and some of it I can barely fathom. I must admit that sometimes it is pretty hard to look in the eyes of a person who is hurting deeply and tell her that she should keep on believing, that she should keep on entrusting her life to God even though he has allowed so much suffering in her life.

Recently I met a woman whose body is being ravaged by ALS (Lou Gehrig's disease) even as she endures the taunts of a cruel husband and the despair of a daughter who has begun cutting herself. I encouraged her to keep trusting God with her suffering, to keep believing that he will use it for something good, knowing even as I said the words that they might sound simplistic in the face of such pain. But deep in my soul I know it is true, and it is not at all simplistic. It is the most significant truth in the universe, so I said it. And I say it to you today too:

Keep on believing . . . because of Christ's love for you expressed on the cross, which makes it possible for you to draw near to God in the darkest times of your life.

Keep on believing . . . because rejection of Christ results in certain—and terrifying—judgment.

Keep on believing . . . because you will be rewarded for your faith in him, and it will be worth everything it costs you.

Keep on believing . . . because as a child of God, it is just who you are.

James 1:12 says, "Blessed is the man who perseveres under trial, because when he has stood the test, he will receive the crown of life that God has promised to those who love him."

Jesus calls us to persevere as we face problems and persecution, and he will be waiting for us on the other side. So keep on believing. It will be worth it. He will be worth it.

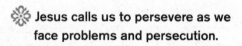

Jesus calls us to persevere as we face problems and persecution.

CHAPTER 8

what are you waiting for?

HEBREWS 11

DAVID AND MATT AND I had been watching a new restaurant being built near where we live. Because we'd eaten at the restaurant before in other cities, our taste memories were making our mouths water as we waited for this new location to open. It opened on a Thursday, and we were there on Saturday night—so excited to give it a try and have this restaurant we love nearby.

We got there a little late for our reservations, so we had to wait, and there was no place to sit. Then we were seated at a table that was at the intersection where all the waiters and waitresses went back and forth into the kitchen. They seated a family with about six kids behind us, and they kept pushing their chairs back into David's chair. And the food was . . . fine. We left with our sense of anticipation having descended into disappointment.

Do you know what it is like to wait for something and be disappointed?

Have you ever anticipated the visit of some old friends and then when they came, you discovered you didn't have much in common anymore, and you

What is it that you are waiting for? Do you think it will bring the satisfaction you're anticipating?

ended up waiting for them to leave? Have you ever bought anything from a catalog or online and anxiously waited for that package to arrive in the mail, only to discover that the fabric wasn't what you had hoped, or it didn't make you look as stunning as you had imagined? Did you save and wait for years to go on the cruise of your dreams, only to spend five nauseating days throwing up over the side of the boat?

We've waited for and then been disappointed by a lot of things, haven't we? Some of them are silly, but others are serious. Some of you may have waited for what seemed like forever to get married, but it didn't turn out at all like you had hoped. Perhaps you spent years planning and preparing for a career that ultimately proved unsatisfying, or a retirement that has ended up being tedious.

What are you hoping for as you look toward the future? What you hope for reflects what you value and what you believe and whom you love. Your hopes reveal the deepest longings of your heart as you look toward the future. What is it that you are waiting for? Do you think it will bring the satisfaction you're anticipating?

The important question for us to ask and answer is, How can we place our hopes not on something that will disappoint us but on Someone who will never disappoint us?

FAITH DEFINED

Hebrews 11 begins by telling us what faith is. It says that faith is "being sure of what we hope for and certain of what we do not see" (verse 1).

Typically when we say we "hope" for something, we're saying that we're not sure it is going to happen, but we want it to. We have no sense of confidence that it will come about. Of course, what we're really talking about is wishful thinking, not biblical hope.

There is nothing uncertain about biblical hope. It speaks of something that is certain but not yet realized. We haven't experienced it yet, but there is no question that it will happen. There is no risk involved in placing our hopes on biblical promises. We can be sure of what we hope for and certain of what we do not see. Biblical hope is certain and real; we just can't see it yet with our physical eyes.

Faith is being convinced that the promises of God we have placed our hopes in are true. It is stepping out to follow a God we have never seen with our eyes or heard with our ears, trusting a reality that the collective voice of the world says does not exist and does not matter. Faith is believing that there is something more durable, more dependable, and more delightful than anything in this world. Faith is believing that something more can be found only in God—and then living like we believe it.

There is nothing uncertain about biblical hope. It speaks of something that is certain but not yet realized.

FAITH DEMONSTRATED

So if faith is the substance of what we hope for, what were the people described in Hebrews 11 hoping for? Let's look at each of them, asking this question: What was the substance of what they were hoping for—the essence of their faith?

Hope for God's Purity (11:4)

> *By faith Abel offered God a better sacrifice than Cain did. By faith he was commended as a righteous man, when God spoke well of his offerings. And by faith he still speaks, even though he is dead.* (HEBREWS 11:4)

Abel grew up in the household of those famous sinners, Adam and Eve. And in a practice that had begun before he was born, when God killed an animal and made garments of skin for Adam and Eve to cover their bodies and their shame, Abel learned that a blood sacrifice was needed to cover sin. In Genesis 4:3-4, we read Abel's story: "In the course of time Cain brought some of the fruits of the soil as an offering to the LORD. But Abel brought fat portions from some of the firstborn of his flock. The LORD looked with favor on Abel and his offering."

Why was Abel's offering so pleasing to God? Because he brought the best he had to offer, from a heart of obedience. His offering reflected an acknowledgment of his sin and his desire for restored purity before God.

We know what it is like to hope for God's purity, don't we? Because even though we've experienced the joy and freedom that come from God's free and lavish forgiveness, the reality is that sin has left behind some stains and scars on our lives that didn't just disappear when we were forgiven. Stains of disgrace left by bad choices. Scars of deep wounds engraved by the sins of others against us. What we're waiting for, what we're longing for, is for those stains and scars to be removed. And one day they will be. The day is coming when we'll be given new bodies and new minds and new emotions that are free from the markings sin has left on us. And that day will be worth waiting for.

Like all the people we read about in Hebrews 11, Abel got a taste of what he was waiting for here and now. He experienced the joy of knowing that his sin was covered when he offered his acceptable sacrifice. But the fullness of what he was hoping for did not come until the next life, in heaven.

And it is the same for us. If we expect to get everything we are hoping for in this life, we will be disappointed. But if we are willing to wait, heaven will provide the fulfillment of our deepest longings, everything we have waited for.

If we expect to get everything we are hoping for in this life, we will be disappointed. But if we are willing to wait, heaven will provide the fulfillment of our deepest longings, everything we have waited for.

Hope for God's Pleasure

The next person of faith we read about in Hebrews 11 is Enoch. Enoch's story, found in Genesis 5:18-24, is very short. We don't know all that much about him except that he is a standout in a long genealogy. He stands out for a couple of reasons—first, because he "walked with God." For all the other descendents in the long list in Genesis 5, we read that so-and-so "lived" X number of years. But it says that Enoch "walked with God" three hundred years. There's a big difference between walking with God and merely living. Second, for all the other descendants on the list, it says, "then he died." But for Enoch, we read that "God took him away." He never experienced physical death. He walked with God on the same path, at the same pace, toward the same place.

> *By faith Enoch was taken from this life, so that he did not experience death; he could not be found, because God had taken him away. For before he was taken, he was commended as one who pleased God. And without faith it is impossible to please God, because anyone who comes to him must believe that he exists and that he rewards those who earnestly seek him.* (HEBREWS 11:5-6)

Wow, to be commended as one who pleases God!

Did you know that we have the ability to please God? We have the ability to bring a smile to the face of the Creator of the universe! We can do so as we walk with him in faith, simply and consistently—talking with him, listening to him, sharing our lives with him, not running ahead of him or dragging our feet in what he has called us to do. And by walking with him, diligently seeking him, we bring him pleasure.

We get a taste of God's pleasure now as we delight in him and obey him, but later we will experience it in full.

Hope for God's Provision

> *By faith Noah, when warned about things not yet seen, in holy fear built an ark to save his family. By his faith he condemned the world and became heir of the righteousness that comes by faith.* (HEBREWS 11:7)

This verse says that Noah was warned about things not yet seen. Noah had never seen a flood. It's possible he had never seen a thunderstorm. He may have never even seen a raindrop. But he believed God. Remember that biblical hope is based on what God has said, not on what we can see.

And as strongly as he believed that there would be judgment on the earth by a flood, he also believed that God would provide a way of escaping that judgment, a way of salvation. Noah had confidence in God's provision of an ark that would protect him from the judgment that was about to fall upon the earth in the form of raindrops.

Likewise, God has promised salvation to all who believe in him, so we need not be destroyed by the coming judgment for sin. In Hebrews 9:28 we read, "Christ was sacrificed once to take away the sins of many people; and he will appear a second time, not to bear sin, but to bring salvation to those who are waiting for him." God has provided everything we need now for salvation, and when he returns for us, that salvation will be complete. But while he brings salvation to those who have come to him for it, he will also bring judgment to those who have rejected his offer. Judgment will then fall on the earth, and next time it won't be rain; it will be fire. But God has provided an ark of safety—Jesus—so that we might be saved.

Judgment will then fall on the earth, and next time it won't be rain; it will be fire. But God has provided an ark of safety–Jesus–so that we might be saved.

Hope for God's Place (11:8-10)

By faith Abraham, when called to go to a place he would later receive as his inheritance, obeyed and went, even though he did not know where he was going. By faith he made his home in the promised land like a stranger in a foreign country; he lived in tents, as did Isaac and Jacob, who were heirs with him of the same promise. For he was looking forward to the city with foundations, whose architect and builder is God. (HEBREWS 11:8-10)

Abraham left a place of idol worship and paganism because he believed what God said about the place God would give to him. Did he leave everything and move right in and make himself at home? Well, no, not exactly. He made his home in the Promised Land "like a stranger in a foreign country." He lived in tents, as did his son and his son's son. In fact, the only land Abraham ever owned in Canaan was a cave in which he buried his wife, Sarah.

That would be like God telling you that he has given you the country of Costa Rica. So you hop on the next plane and go there, and you spend the rest of your life there living in a camper. Your kids live in the next camper, and their kids live in the next camper over. You move from place to place with no home, no citizenship, no rights—always an outsider, never fitting in.

But this passage says that Abraham was "looking forward to the city with foundations, whose architect and builder is God." Evidently, Abraham's greatest hopes and dreams for a homeland were invested not in earthly Canaan but in his heavenly homeland, a city with foundations. No more moving from place to place in temporary lodging—this city would be designed in God's mind and built with his hands.

I imagine that as Abraham stepped into that heavenly city he had hoped for and dreamed of, he must have said, "Heaven was worth waiting for!" No disappointment, no regret. And today, based on faith in what God has said, we longingly look forward to our heavenly home that is being prepared for us. And when we get there, we, too, will say, "Heaven was worth the wait! Jesus is worth all the waiting!"

Do you look forward to heaven because you see it as the place where you will finally feel completely at home? Or have you become too comfortable right here? Have you so settled for being a stranger and an alien here that you have been sapped of your longing for heaven and hardly even realize it?

Would you set your sights higher, adjust your perspective, retrain your appetite for heaven?

Hope for God's Promised Child

> *By faith Abraham, even though he was past age—and Sarah herself was barren—was enabled to become a father because he considered him faithful who had made the promise. And so from this one man, and he as good as dead, came descendants as numerous as the stars in the sky and as countless as the sand on the seashore.* (HEBREWS 11:11-12)

Do you know what it is like to long for a child? Then you have a taste of what it was like for Abraham and Sarah to long, not just for any child, but for a child whom God himself had audibly promised to them. Month after month, when Sarah's period started, they must have felt the wave of disappointment. But imagine what it must have been like when Sarah stopped having periods altogether. To continue to hope for a child—even one child, let alone descendants as numerous as the stars in the sky—must have seemed ridiculous and beyond reason. And it was. Except that it was a hope based on God's promise. And God's promises are always sure. Biblical hope is based on what God has said, not on what we can see.

Biblical hope is based on what God has said, not on what we can see.

And so finally, much to the old couple's amusement, Sarah's belly began to grow, and sure enough, Isaac was born. But Abraham's progeny didn't stop there. The truth is, you and I are now descendants of Abraham, part of the "descendants as numerous as the stars in the sky." Romans 4:11 tells us that Abraham is "the father of all who believe." Abraham and Sarah placed their hope—sometimes impatiently and sometimes disobediently, but ultimately in full faith—in God for their family. And I think they would tell you, "It was worth the wait."

Hope for God's Power

It wasn't just any kind of power Abraham was hoping for. He was hoping for resurrection power.

> *By faith Abraham, when God tested him, offered Isaac as a sacrifice. He who had received the promises was about to sacrifice his one and only son, even though God had said to him, "It is through Isaac that your offspring will be reckoned." Abraham reasoned that God could raise the dead, and figuratively speaking, he did receive Isaac back from death.* (HEBREWS 11:17-19)

Imagine the joy in Abraham and Sarah's household when Isaac was born! Isaac's very name means laughter. And then imagine what it must have been like for Abraham to hear God calling to him. Abraham answered in anticipation, "Here I am" (Genesis 22:1). How his heart must have sunk, how he must have felt physically sickened by what he heard when God said, in essence, "Take your son Isaac and put him to death by your own hand and then burn up his body" (Genesis 22:2).

Genesis records that "early the next morning Abraham got up and saddled his donkey" (22:3) and headed up the mountain with young Isaac at his side. He must have wept as he walked. And yet this passage in Hebrews reveals to us what gave Abraham the strength to keep going, what gave him the confidence to tell his servants, "*We* will worship and then *we* will come back to you" (22:5, emphasis added). It was Abraham's confident hope in God's resurrection power.

God had said Abraham's descendants would come specifically through Isaac, not just any son, so if God was asking him to kill Isaac, Abraham reasoned that God must have been planning to raise Isaac from the dead. Abraham knew that even death could not frustrate God's purposes and plan—that God's promise is sure.

Do you also long for God's resurrection power? We experience Christ's resurrection power now when we come to life spiritually and when he empowers us to overcome sin. But the day is coming when we will experience bodily resurrection as we rise to meet him in the air.

Abraham knew that even death could not frustrate God's purposes and plan–that God's promise is sure.

Now if you're like me, there are some days when you can hardly believe that you believe that, let alone say it out loud. But if you don't believe it, then frankly, you have no genuine hope for the future; this life is all there is. If you do believe it, based on the fact that God has promised it, then the day will come when you will rise from your grave to meet Jesus in the air. And you will say, "Jesus, you have been worth the wait!"

Hope for God's Promises

What was Isaac hoping for? The most precious things Isaac had inherited from his father, Abraham, were the promises of God and his faith in them. And just as Abraham had passed along the promises to Isaac, the joy of Isaac's life was passing along these promises to his own sons. "By faith Isaac blessed Jacob and Esau in regard to their future" (11:20).

Isaac hoped for God's promises to be fulfilled. Isaac placed his hopes for the future on God's future fulfillment of those blessings, and he placed his faith in the sovereignty of God. Likewise, the most precious thing we can pass along to our children is our faith in God's promises.

Hope for God's Predetermined Choosing

Isaac had twin sons, Jacob and Esau. Although Jacob was born after Esau, he tricked Esau out of his firstborn birthright, and then he tricked his father, who had lost his eyesight, into passing the blessing on to him. And just as Jacob had done some switcheroo in regard to obtaining the blessing, there was some last-minute switching as he prepared to offer his blessing to his own sons and grandsons.

As a way of honoring Joseph, Jacob offered a blessing to each of Joseph's sons along with each of his own sons, basically "promoting" these two to the status of sons rather than grandsons. Genesis 48:13-14 sets the scene of the switch: "Joseph took both of them, Ephraim on his right toward Israel's [Jacob's] left hand and Manasseh on his left toward Israel's right hand, and brought them close to him. But Israel reached out his right hand and put it on Ephraim's head, though he was the younger, and crossing his arms, he put his left hand on Manasseh's head, even though Manasseh was the firstborn." Jacob's blessing, at God's prompting, took on prophetic significance, as Ephraim would be the more influential of the two and his tribe the dominant one of the ten northern tribes.

So Jacob hoped for God's predestination—God's ultimate choosing about whom he would call and whom he would use. God does not choose as we choose, based on talent or looks or birthright. God chooses as he wills, and his choosing does not always make sense to us. Sometimes we don't understand why he chooses someone we see as less gifted or less qualified to fill a particular role.

We experience being chosen by God for callings here on earth, but our ultimate hope is in God's choosing us to be his forever. When we see him someday, we will praise him and thank him for choosing us to spend eternity with him.

God does not choose as we choose, based on talent or looks or birthright. God chooses as he wills, and his choosing does not always make sense to us.

Hope for the Fulfillment of God's Prophecies

What was it Joseph hoped for as he spent all those years as a slave in Egypt, then for years as he was forgotten in prison, and then as he became prime minister of Egypt? Joseph hoped for God's prophecies to be fulfilled, specifically the prophecies that his family would one day possess the land of Canaan.

> *By faith Joseph, when his end was near, spoke about the exodus of the Israelites from Egypt and gave instructions about his bones.* (HEBREWS 11:22)

In Genesis 50:24-25 we read, "Joseph said to his brothers, 'I am about to die. But God will surely come to your aid and take you up out of this land to the land he promised on oath to Abraham, Isaac and Jacob.' And Joseph made the sons of Israel swear an oath and said, 'God will surely come to your aid, and then you must carry my bones up from this place.'"

He remembered what God had said to Abram: "Know for certain that your descendants will be strangers in a country not their own, and they will be enslaved and mistreated four hundred years. But I will punish the nation they serve as slaves, and afterward they will come out with great possessions" (Genesis 15:13-14).

Joseph believed strongly in this prophecy, and he wanted to make sure that his bones went with the Israelites when they left Egypt (four hundred years later). Sure enough, Exodus 13:19 tells us, "Moses took the bones of Joseph with him because Joseph had made the sons of Israel swear an oath."

I find it amazing that Joseph could hold on to the prophecies of the Promised Land, considering he left home at age seventeen and lived in Egypt until he died. Somehow in those first seventeen years he took hold of God's promise and never let go, and he longed to see it fulfilled. Perhaps he had that longing all those years, or perhaps it all came back to him when his brothers bowed down to him and he remembered the dream he'd had as a child that this would happen. Perhaps then he remembered his father's words about the Promised Land and he longed, once again, to see God's promises and prophecies fulfilled.

We have that longing, too, don't we? We can look back at Scripture and see the prophecies that have been fulfilled—especially in the coming and crucifixion of Jesus. But there are so many prophecies that have not been fulfilled yet. The prophecies of Jesus' return. The lion lying down with the lamb. Jesus on the throne before our eyes. No more wars. No more tears. No more pain. We are still waiting and hoping. These promises will be fulfilled, and it will be worth the wait.

Hope for God's Prize

Even though most of us have seen *The Ten Commandments* with Charlton Heston or specials about ancient Egypt on the Discovery Channel, it is still pretty hard for us to fathom that culture's wealth and progress and power. So it is hard for us to grasp what Moses walked away from when he chose to leave behind the life of a prince to Pharaoh.

> *By faith Moses, when he had grown up, refused to be known as the son of Pharaoh's daughter. He chose to be mistreated along with the people of God rather than to enjoy the pleasures of sin for a short time. He regarded disgrace for the sake of Christ as of greater value than the treasures of Egypt, because he was looking ahead to his reward. By faith he left Egypt, not fearing the king's anger; he persevered because he saw him who is invisible. By faith he kept the Passover and the sprinkling of blood, so that the destroyer of the firstborn would not touch the firstborn of Israel.* (HEBREWS 11:24-28)

What was Moses hoping for that caused him to walk away from wealth and privilege? Moses hoped for God's prize. Moses had his eyes and his heart set on something better than the treasures of Egypt—the reward that awaited him in heaven. Moses was willing to pass up temporary pleasure now for the lasting, ultimate pleasure of God's reward.

For some reason we have been afraid to talk about rewards in the church—afraid it will rob from us the joy of obedience, of loving and serving God for himself without expecting anything in return. But the truth of Scripture is that faithfulness here will be rewarded in heaven. Jesus said we should be happy when we are persecuted for his sake, because "great is your reward in heaven" (Matthew 5:12). Great is our reward. Perhaps because we don't understand it, we devalue it. But to be too "spiritual" to want the reward God has promised is to be more spiritual than Jesus, who held out the promise to us as a comfort and a motivation.

If you are persevering in your faith through suffering or persecution, then consider God's promise of reward. It will be great. And it will be worth what it has cost you. If you are serving Jesus by serving the needs of others, then rest in your anticipation of God's promised reward.

Hope for God's Protection

> *By faith the people passed through the Red Sea as on dry land; but when the Egyptians tried to do so, they were drowned. By faith the walls of Jericho fell, after the people had marched around them for seven days. By faith the pros-*

> *titute Rahab, because she welcomed the spies, was not killed with those who were disobedient.* (HEBREWS 11:29-31)

The people of Israel were like most of us. They wanted to do whatever it took to be safe and secure. As they walked toward the Red Sea and as they marched around Jericho, they longed, as we do, for God's protection. So did Rahab, the prostitute in Jericho who let the Israelite spies stay in her home. She knew the Israelites were about to attack and conquer Jericho, and she wanted to be safe from attack. The people of Israel and Rahab hoped for God's protection.

We hope for that too, don't we? But do you know what it is like to hope for God to protect you and then to feel like he has not? I do. I remember about a year after Hope died, a question in my group Bible study directed us to read Psalm 91 and express how it had been true in our lives.

It says, "If you make the Most High your dwelling—even the LORD, who is my refuge—then no harm will befall you, no disaster will come near your tent. For he will command his angels concerning you to guard you in all your ways; they will lift you up in their hands, so that you will not strike your foot against a stone" (verses 9-12).

And I just had to say what I thought: "I don't get how this is true. It feels to me that God did not protect my family."

Do you ever read something like that in the Bible and think, "That's not true!"? We know in our heads that the Bible is true, but sometimes, based on our experiences and our understanding, we can't seem to reconcile it with reality. It is then that we have to dig deeper for understanding and clarity. God's Word is solid, so we know it must be our thinking or theology that is on shaky ground.

I'll tell you how I was able to make some sense of this psalm. It is based on this truth: God is much more interested in the life of your soul than the life of your body. Your earthly body is going to die. Your eternal soul is going to live forever. His ability to protect your soul eternally from judgment and death is more significant than his ability to

God is much more interested in the life of your soul than the life of your body. Your earthly body is going to die. Your eternal soul is going to live forever.

protect your body from disease or attack or death. It doesn't seem or feel as significant to us, because we are trapped in these bodies in this time and it is so hard for us to imagine our eternal future with him. So we try to apply his promises for the protection of our souls to our bodies, and we're left disappointed.

God often protects his children from harm in this life, but ultimately he has protected us from eternal harm—his wrath that will fall on the earth to judge sin. Judgment is coming. But he will protect us from judgment. Those of us who hide ourselves in Christ are protected for eternity, so we can rest while we wait.

Hope for God's Perfection

There is a great variety of people and hopes represented in the list of people described in verses 32-38. But there is one group of people for whom we are told exactly what they were hoping for—the women described in verse 35. "Women received back their dead, raised to life again. Others were tortured and refused to be released, so that they might gain a better resurrection."

What could be better than having the one you love who has died raised back to life again? I'll tell you what–a resurrection that is more than mere rehabilitation or resuscitation.

What could be better than having the one you love who has died raised back to life again? What could be better than escaping being tortured for your faith? I'll tell you what—a resurrection that is more than mere rehabilitation or resuscitation. Those who were raised back to life again still died eventually. (What a bummer to have to die a second time!) These women had their hearts set on a better resurrection, a resurrection that would be for eternity.

These women hoped for God's perfection—not just a temporary fix to the problem of death, but an eternal one. Throughout history, believers have experienced God's supernatural power in many ways, but the ultimate miracle we long for is the "better resurrection," which is eternal.

What could be better than the one you love being resuscitated after the accident? What could be better than seeing the one you love walk again or work again or wake up again?

Resurrection. A better resurrection. It doesn't necessarily feel better at the time. It feels like loss. But by faith we see that for the believer, the future holds a better resurrection.

I don't think the hope of a better resurrection had ever been as important to me as it was the night we sensed that our son Gabriel was succumbing to the fatal effects of his syndrome. Matt had already gone to bed, so we woke him and told him we thought Gabe might die during the night and we wanted him to have the chance to say good-bye. Then we put Gabe in our bed between us and thanked God for his life. I pulled out my Bible and opened it to 1 Corinthians 15 and turned to Gabe, saying, "Gabe, do you want to hear about the resurrection?"

When we face the grave, as we all will, all the religious talk about resurrection becomes more than just talk. It was all too real for me in that moment—and it was of supreme importance. In those hours saying good-bye to Gabe, I needed to reaffirm that the resurrection is real and that it is our solid hope. So I began to read out loud, "If corpses can't be raised, then Christ wasn't, because he was indeed dead. And if Christ weren't raised, then all you're doing is wandering about in the dark, as lost as ever. . . . If all we get out of Christ is a little inspiration for a few short years, we're a pretty sorry lot. But the truth is that Christ *has* been raised up, the first in a long legacy of those who are going to leave the cemeteries. . . . It's resurrection, resurrection, always resurrection, that undergirds what I do and say, the way I live" (1 Corinthians 15:16-20, 32, *The Message*).

Resurrection will be the perfection we have waited for. Oh, how I long for that day! I believe it is really coming and that it will be worth waiting for.

FAITH'S DISAPPOINTMENT?

So let's take an honest assessment. Did these people get what they were hoping for?

The answer is given plainly in the first part of verse 13: "All these people were still living by faith when they died. They did not receive the things promised." Then in verse 39 the answer to our question is repeated: "These were all commended for their faith, yet none of them received what had been promised."

There it is. They died and they didn't get it. And if they didn't get what they were hoping for, how can we expect to? What are we waiting for if we can't expect to get what we are hoping for?

But that's not the end of the story. Let's continue in verse 13: "They did not receive the things promised; they only saw them and welcomed them from a distance."

The truth is, they didn't receive what was promised in this life. But they received far better than anything they could have ever imagined in the next. And so will we.

What was it they saw in the distance that was the fulfillment of their hopes? What was promised that they were willing to wait for?

A Better Promise

They all died in faith, still waiting for the promised Messiah.

These two people of faith knew there was a Savior coming, but they could only see him from a distance, and they couldn't make him out clearly. They looked forward in faith to the coming and crucifixion of Jesus, and they depended on the Cross for salvation in the same way that we look back at it in faith for salvation. We have the benefit of seeing it more clearly than they could.

A Better Place

They all died as strangers in this world, confident of a heavenly home.

> *They admitted that they were aliens and strangers on earth. People who say such things show that they are looking for a country of their own. If they had been thinking of the country they had left, they would have had opportunity to return. Instead, they were longing for a better country—a heavenly one.* (HEBREWS 11:13-16)

Abraham may have died with no home and with only a cave to his name. Moses may have died having never set foot in the Promised Land. But they died confident of a better place—a better country than Canaan, a better home than the Promised Land.

A Better Privilege

They all died commended for their faith by God.

> *Therefore God is not ashamed to be called their God.* (HEBREWS 11:16)

> *These were all commended for their faith.* (HEBREWS 11:39)

Because they desired this better heavenly country, they persevered in their faith, even when they couldn't see their future resting place. And through their perseverance, they received the privilege of being commended by God.

What a privilege—for God to say about you, "She's mine. I'm her God." Can you see him like a proud papa after his son wins the football game or his daughter shines at the dance recital? "I'm so proud of her and her faith; she has persevered through difficulty and disappointment; she waited for me."

Do you wonder if you'll be disappointed if you place all your hopes in God's promises? Think again. Draw a picture in your mind of that day when God tells you for all to hear, "Well done. I'm so proud of you! You're mine!"

A Better Plan

They will all live again with us, fulfilling God's plan of redeeming people for himself.

> *God had planned something better for us so that only together with us would they be made perfect.* (HEBREWS 11:40)

"God had planned something better. . . ." When we look at what these people endured, most of us would probably say that their lives are not necessarily what we have in mind for our lives. But we have to be willing to let go of the plans we have made for our lives so that we can embrace God's plans for us—better plans than whatever we are tempted to hold on to.

Deep in the heart of God, long ago, he began working out his plan to buy back those he had created through the death of his Son. And he has made it possible for us to know him and love him and live with him forever. What a beautiful, magnificent, holy plan!

We have to be willing to let go of the plans we have made for our lives so that we can embrace God's plans for us—better plans than whatever we are tempted to hold on to.

FAITH DELAYED

So if it is God's plan that we wait and hope as he works out his plan in his timing, what do you and I do while we wait and hope? We find instructions for that in several passages outside of Hebrews.

We Groan as We Wait

> *We know that the whole creation has been groaning as in the pains of childbirth right up to the present time. Not only so, but we ourselves, who have the firstfruits of the Spirit, groan inwardly as we wait eagerly for our adoption as sons, the redemption of our bodies. For in this hope we were saved. But hope that is seen is no hope at all. Who hopes for what he already has? But if we hope for what we do not yet have, we wait for it patiently.* (ROMANS 8:22-25)

The very nature of hope is that we are waiting for something we have not yet seen or experienced. And none of us likes to wait. When we are waiting for something wonderful, we are eager with anticipation. But in our eagerness, as we wait for what God has prepared for us, we groan.

When we are waiting for something wonderful, we are eager with anticipation. But in our eagerness, as we wait for what God has prepared for us, we groan.

I seem to go through times when I especially feel this sense of groaning inwardly. Do you? I remember last December going through a period of several days when I seemed profoundly aware of the hurts of the world around me. It wasn't just my own seasonal sorrow that weighed on me. I get lots of letters and e-mail from hurting people who have read my books, and I feel their sorrow as I read their letters and interact with them. All of that was on my mind when I turned on the TV. I saw a preview for a movie that involved child sexual abuse and a story on the news of a family whose house had burned down. Then, to top it all off—and you'll now discover how pathetic I really am—I was driving along and saw a beautiful dog that had been hit by a car, dead on the side of the road.

Doesn't the pain and suffering and sadness in the world sometimes cause you to groan inwardly? to ache for the hurts that people experience, that all of creation experiences as we wait for redemption? Don't you ever wonder when all this hurting will end? Why doesn't God just come now and take us out of this world that is so full of pain?

Verse 22 says that "the whole creation has been groaning as in the pains of childbirth."

Now I remember the pains of childbirth. I have never been out to be a hero when it comes to childbirth, and my motto has been, "Bring on the epidural, the earlier the better." But when I was in labor with Matt and it wasn't progressing, my doctor thought the epidural might be inhibiting my pushing, so he gave instructions to turn the epidural off. They did. And for a couple of hours I pushed with no epidural. I don't remember much about it actually, except muttering to myself, "Remember how bad this feels and DO NOT allow yourself to get into this situation again!"

The groans of childbirth, however, are quickly forgotten when we hold that beautiful child in our arms. It has been worth those nine months of waiting, worth the pain of delivery. And that's how it will be when we are finally in the presence of God. The groaning and anticipation will be over, and we will say, "It was worth the wait. Jesus, you are worth all the waiting!"

Have you wondered sometimes if something is wrong with you or if there's something deficient in your faith because you just can't share in the happy-all-the-time religion some seem to have? When you find yourself groaning because of the death and destruction and disease and depression and deprivation in this world, and you find deep inside an intense longing for all of it to be erased and made right, that is a sacred longing, placed deep within you because of the hope that you have. You have hope for the day that, as it says in Romans 8:21, "The creation itself will be liberated from its bondage to decay and brought into the glorious freedom of the children of God."

We Fix Our Eyes on What We Cannot See

> *So we fix our eyes not on what is seen, but on what is unseen. For what is seen is temporary, but what is unseen is eternal. . . . Therefore we are always confident and know that as long as we are at home in the body we are away from the Lord. We live by faith, not by sight.* (2 CORINTHIANS 4:18; 5:6-7)

We have never seen Christ, and yet we fix our eyes of faith on him whom we have not seen, and we believe. We have never seen bodies rise up out of graves. And yet we fix our eyes of faith on the Scripture, and we believe. We have never seen a place called heaven and cannot find it on a map or in the universe, and we can't imagine what it will be like. Yet we fix our eyes of faith on God's promises, and we believe. Biblical hope provides the special "glasses" that enable us to see the invisible.

We Make It Our Goal to Please Him

> *We are confident, I say, and would prefer to be away from the body and at home with the Lord. So we make it our goal to please him, whether we are at home in the body or away from it.* (2 CORINTHIANS 5:8-9)

Real hope is not about wishing for the best in this world. Real hope causes us to long for another world. That is what hope is meant to do—to give us a deep, unquenchable longing for heaven.

I remember reading this verse shortly before I discovered I was pregnant with Gabriel. It seemed to jump out at me and take hold of me, guiding me through that confusing time. And it has been my guiding verse ever since. I can't control the world around me or what happens to my family and me. But this verse shows me what I *can* do, where I can put my focus and my energies as I wait.

Really, it is simple. As we wait for heaven, we throw everything we have and everything we are into this singular aim. We aim to please God. It is more important than if we survive or if we die. We set our sights on pleasing God.

When hard things come (and they will) and we wonder what to do, we make it our goal to please him in how we respond. When our husband tells us he no longer wants to be married and wants a divorce, we throw ourselves into pleasing God. When we feel the sting of undeserved criticism, the fearfulness of being alone, the weight of overwhelming responsibility, or perhaps the aimlessness of lack of purpose or significance, we make it our aim to please him. That is what we do while we wait.

And it will be worth it. He will be worth everything your sacrificial obedience has cost you and will cost you.

Hope allows us to see beyond the darkness as we fix our eyes on what we cannot see. Real hope is not about wishing for the best in this world. Real hope causes us to long for another world. That is what hope is meant to do—to give us a deep, unquenchable longing for heaven.

So what are you waiting for? What keeps you getting up in the morning? What drives you? What are you looking forward to?

I hope it will be worth it. I do.

But I also know that everything good in this life—the best things in this life—are just a taste of what we will experience in a richer and fuller way in heaven.

So many of us have faced so much disappointment here, haven't we? But faith tells us that we can be confident of what we can't see. We can rest in knowing that heaven will not disappoint us as life does.

> *Compared to what's coming, living conditions around here seem like a stopover in an unfurnished shack, and we're tired of it! We've been given a glimpse of the real thing, our true home, our resurrection bodies! The Spirit of God whets our appetite by giving us a taste of what's ahead. He puts a little of heaven in our hearts so that we'll never settle for less.* (2 CORINTHIANS 5:4-5, THE MESSAGE)

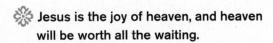

Jesus is the joy of heaven, and heaven will be worth all the waiting.

CHAPTER 9

what is your obsession?

HEBREWS 12:1-24

I'M NOT SURE I'M qualified to write about Hebrews 12. The writer draws a picture of living out our faith as if it is a race. So you should know up front that my personal racing career ended before it began in fifth grade.

Remember those awful presidential physical fitness tests? I think that is what we were doing. And you have to understand that my boyfriend in fifth grade, Scott Hanberry, was a great runner. (Are you still out there, Scott Hanberry, and are you still running?) His sister was my best buddy, and I would go with their family on Saturdays to the all-city track competitions that Scott would run in and often win. Running was a big deal to him.

I can picture where we were on the school yard at David Brewer Elementary School when all the fifth-grade girls lined up and took off. It is one of those experiences etched in my emotional memory. Mostly I remember the look on Scott's face as I crossed the finish line next to last, way behind the pack. He looked so disappointed, and I felt humiliated.

I have struggled with my weight for most of my life, including during my

> I want Jesus to be the center of my life, the focus of my thoughts, the object of my passion, the definer of my identity, the source of my significance, the supplier of my happiness, my definition of beauty.

childhood, and my poor race finish seemed to rub in the reality that my weight was a hindrance to my ability to run fast.

To tell you the truth, I've spent much more energy running toward the refrigerator than on a racetrack. If I'm painfully and awkwardly honest with you, I have to admit that I am obsessed with food. I love breakfast. I love lunch. I love dinner. I love to have a snack at about ten and to eat a few tortilla chips while I'm fixing dinner. And what is the point of a day that doesn't end with a bowl of ice cream?

But my love affair with food has not served me well. It has made me mostly miserable—either miserable from depriving myself to try to lose weight and keep it off or miserable because I'm not depriving myself and my weight is creeping up and my clothes are getting tighter.

I'm embarrassed when I realize that while most people in the world are trying to figure out how to get enough food to eat to survive, here I am struggling to figure out how to eat less in the abundance that surrounds me. Something is way out of whack.

A while ago I got sick of myself—not just sick of my reflection in the mirror that made me want to hide, but sick of having my thoughts and emotions dominated by food. I don't want food and my weight to be this important, this significant in my life. It just isn't an investment worthy of so much energy. So I have been on a journey to put food and weight management in its proper place in my life. I don't want to be obsessed with it. I don't want it to consume so much of my energy and emotion.

Would I love to be thin? Of course. What woman doesn't want that? But I don't want the desire for thinness to drive me. And I don't want the absence of thinness to have the power to destroy me.

I want something else—some*one* else—to take center stage in my thoughts and emotions. I want a different obsession, a better obsession. I want Jesus to be the center of my life, the focus of my thoughts, the object of my passion, the definer of my identity, the source of my significance, the supplier of my happiness, my definition of beauty. I want Jesus to satisfy my appetites and longings. Not food. Not achieving and maintaining a particular number on the scale or a certain clothing size.

So there you have my true confession of my embarrassing obsession. And if you also struggle with this, then you know that it is a painful thing to talk about, because it is mixed up inside our heads and hearts with so much shame and embarrassment and feelings of failure and fear.

But I am willing to share this because I know I'm not the only one with an obsession. What are you obsessed with? Is it your weight or appearance? your house? your children? your vacation home? your reputation? your relationship with a certain person? Are you so obsessed with something that happened in the past that you can't move forward? Are you obsessed with collecting what you think you'll need to ensure a comfortable future? Are you simply obsessed with yourself—your own needs and concerns and interests?

Now wait a minute, I can hear you saying. *What is wrong with taking pride in my appearance, enjoying my children, making a comfortable home?* Absolutely nothing. It's just that we have such a hard time keeping these things in proper balance, don't we?

It's not that what we want is bad. It's that we want it too much. Our desire becomes a demand, and we find ourselves off track, obsessed with so many lesser things than Jesus himself.

It's not that what we want is bad. It's that we want it too much. Our desire becomes a demand, and we find ourselves off track, obsessed with so many lesser things than Jesus himself.

Now I know that for some of you reading this, something that is very important to you has come to your mind, and you're already building your defense for why your fascination and dedication to whatever-it-is is fine and not out of line, and why don't I just get off your case?

Here's the bottom line of Hebrews 12: We must take stock of our ambitions and allegiances and affections to make sure that Jesus is at the center of our lives, in his rightful place. We want to be obsessed with him, not merely affiliated with him or interested in him or associated with him. We want to be united with him, to give ourselves to him, letting go of whatever keeps us from him so we can run toward him.

Our ability to run is not dependent on our physical ability but on how much we keep our focus on the greatest racer of all time—Jesus himself.

We have a singular aim to crossing the finish line of faith. Our ability to run is not dependent on our physical ability but on how much we keep our focus on the greatest racer of all time—Jesus himself—who ran the perfect race of faith and now waits for us, encouraging us, providing us with the energy and example we need to run well. It is our longing for him, our love for him, and our obsession with him that prod us to get moving, to enter the race of faith, and to complete the race.

THROW OFF HINDRANCES

Since we are surrounded by such a great cloud of witnesses, let us throw off everything that hinders and the sin that so easily entangles, and let us run with perseverance the race marked out for us. (HEBREWS 12:1)

When we read this verse, we might quickly conclude that the message is, Since all these saints we read about in Hebrews 11 are in the gallery watching us, our goal should be to not disappoint these "witnesses." But what does a witness in a legal setting do? She testifies about her own experience.

So when we read that these people of faith are a "great cloud of witnesses," it doesn't mean we'd better run a good race because they're watching. The point is not that they are looking at us, but that we are to look at them and listen to them. They ran their race of faith well, and their jerseys have been retired, and now we are on the racetrack. As we look at them and listen to them, they inspire and encourage us to run our races well. They "witness" to us what living by faith means and how it is worthwhile. They are examples, not onlookers.

As we look at them and listen to them, we see the value of persevering in faith. That is what they did. They all faced tremendous difficulty and they persevered, staying faithful to the end. And as we look at them, we see the value of placing our hope in God's promises, as they did. They call out to us, testifying that living the life of faith is worth everything it may cost us. Jesus is worth the wait, they say. We believe, as we look at their example, that there is value in placing all our hopes in what God has promised. It worked for them, and it will work for us.

Have you ever been inspired by the godly example of those who have run the race of faith longer or more intensely than you have? Has watching them made you want to pick up your pace, apply yourself more diligently? What do we learn from those who have run the race of faith well?

First, we learn that we're going to have to "throw off everything that hinders and the sin that so easily entangles." We're going to have to get rid of everything that gets tangled in our feet and causes us to fall on our faces, every weight that keeps us from making steady progress in drawing near to God.

What is weighing you down as you try to draw near to God? Is it guilt? anxiety? unforgiveness? For many of the Hebrew people this letter was addressed to, the weight was legalism. They had grown up under so much law-keeping in an effort to be righteous, they had a hard time letting go of it. They were carrying around a weight that they were never meant to carry. The dos and don'ts of religion will suck the life out of the life of faith.

Are you carrying around a load of unmet expectations or unnecessary activity that you were never meant to carry? Would you lay it down, throw it off?

A weight is anything that dampens your enthusiasm for the things of God. It doesn't necessarily have to be a bad thing. What's wrong with watching borderline-trashy reality TV? Nothing perhaps, unless it dampens your passion for godly relationships or godly values. What's wrong with a drink now and then? Nothing perhaps, unless it diminishes your thirst for the milk of the Word or destroys your credibility for sharing the gospel. What is wrong with loving to shop? Nothing perhaps, unless it nurtures your love for the comforts of this life more than your longing for heaven.

Is what you are holding on to a help or a hindrance in your pursuit of drawing near to God?

Is what you are holding on to a help or a hindrance in your pursuit of drawing near to God?

What is the sin that easily entangles you, the sin that you repeatedly fall into, that seems to keep tripping you up? Is it jealousy? envy? criticism? lust? pride? It might be different from the sin that easily trips me up. We each have to identify what that easy-to-fall-into sin is for us so we can make the necessary choices to avoid it next time.

Are you really serious about making some progress in drawing near to God? You will need to turn away from every sin that is tripping you up. You will need to cut away anything and everything that is weighing you down. And the cutting away may be painful.

In my efforts to deal with my weight so I won't be so obsessed with worrying about it, I've figured something out. I can't be making chocolate chip cookies all the time. I love to make chocolate chip cookies. And honestly, it is just as much about eating the dough as it is about eating the cookies. But I've figured out that if I want to manage my weight well, I can't do it.

And it is not just that I can't make the cookies. If I don't want to make the cookies, then I can't buy the chocolate chips and have them calling out to me from my pantry. As Barney Fife said, I have to "nip it in the bud." I can't make a provision for making chocolate chip cookies.

Likewise, I can't make any provision to once again fall into the sins that easily trip me up—such as pride. I know myself well enough to know the settings and situations in which I have repeatedly become entangled in the cords of my own identity. And I don't want to keep falling on my face. So I have to go into those settings and situations prayed up and prepared so I won't fall into this sin again. I can't be casual about it, and I can't set myself up to fall, thinking I'll just be stronger this time. This is what Romans 13:14 means when it says to "make no provision for the flesh in regard to its lusts" (NASB). We can't keep setting ourselves up to fall.

When I was in high school there were several guys in my calculus class who were on the swim team. And when it came time for a really big race, they would shave everything—their legs and their arms, everything. They wore tiny little suits. They covered their heads with swim caps. And they shaved every exposed hair on their bodies, because they didn't want anything to slow them down. They wanted to win the race.

Are you really serious about making some progress in drawing near to God? You will need to turn away from every sin that is tripping you up. You will need to cut away anything and everything that is weighing you down. And the cutting away may be painful. But in truth, it will be a relief. You don't need that extra weight slowing you down from going where you really want to go.

RUN WITH PERSEVERANCE

Once we have cut away the sin that entangles and let go of the weight that slows us, we are to "run with perseverance the race marked out for us." What will it take to run the race of faith with perseverance?

Entrance

We have to choose to respond to the call of God to enter the race. We cannot be content to sit on the sidelines and watch others run. We can't just listen to the radio or sit in the pew and hear about other people who are running. We have to enter the race. It will require some risk and some courage and some obedience, but we have to choose to run. We have to decide that we don't want to stay where we are, as we are, doing what we've been doing, but that we want to make progress in the race of faith.

Energy

God himself supplies the energy as we run our race of faith toward him. He gives us everything we need. As we feed on the fuel of the Word of God, and as the Holy Spirit blows the wind at our backs and fills our lungs with his very breath, we are empowered to run with God-supplied energy.

Endurance

The race will require steadfastness, a steady determination to keep going. Some people start the Christian life with great vigor but then slow down, give up, and eventually collapse. But if we want to complete our race well, we have to keep going even when we're tired, even when the pathway is difficult. With perseverance, and with our eyes riveted on God's sure promises, we keep running our race.

It makes no sense to enter a race we have no desire to complete. Many Christians are content to be saved from hell and then sit down and wait for heaven. Paul spoke of his own fight against this tendency in 1 Corinthians 9:26-27: "I do not run like a man running aimlessly; I do not fight like a man beating the air. No, I beat my body and make it my slave so that after I have preached to others, I myself will not be disqualified for the prize." We run this race with an aim—an aim to endure and finish the race.

Exclusivity

Sometimes this race will be lonely. Sometimes you will wonder why more people are not running with you. Don't think that something is wrong. Jesus said, "Wide is the gate and broad is the road that leads to destruction, and many enter through it. But small is the gate and narrow the road that leads to life, and only a few find it" (Matthew 7:13-14). Many people around us are running races of good works or religiosity, but they aren't running the race of faith. We run the race of faith, recognizing that it may, at times, be a very lonely race.

We each have to run the race that is set before us. I may not be able to run the course your race takes you on, and you may not be able to run mine. But I can finish the course that God has marked out for me, and you can finish the course God has marked out for you. God will equip us to do what he calls us to do. Some of us might sprint and some of us might plod, but we all must persevere.

Don't Look Around

As we persevere, where do we look for the encouragement and example we will need? If we want to run the race of faith to win, we will have to stop looking around so we can look up.

Do you remember the scene in the movie *Chariots of Fire* when Harold Abrahams hires a coach who shows him a film of a recent race he lost? The coach points to the moment in the race when Abrahams took his eyes off the finish line and looked to the side to see where the other racers were. And in that moment, he lost momentum and was beaten.

All great racers know that if you allow yourself to look around at others and evaluate or compare the race they are running, you will be distracted from your own race and it will slow you down. But looking at others is our natural tendency, isn't it? *Her race is easier. . . . She's not even applying herself and yet she seems to be doing so well. . . . She is so far ahead of me; I will never be able to catch up.* Or we think that we're so far ahead of the pack, we need not push ourselves. Don't get distracted by the race others are running. It will only hinder your progress.

We're not competing against each other; we're encouraging each other. We're competing against Satan, the world's system, our own flesh. Let's keep our focus on the race marked out for us, not on those around us.

Don't Look Inward

Other runners may be tempted to spend too much time in self-evaluation. But don't look inward—it will discourage you. If we spend all our time and energy focused on our own resources or lack thereof, on our own issues or limitations, we will become completely discouraged—perhaps to the point that we will simply quit the race.

Don't Look Back

Some of the runners this writer was talking to had begun to look back—at the old ways of Judaism and the old system of the law—and it only delayed their progress. Don't look back; it will slow you down. If you look back longingly at the way things used to be, if you live in the past, you will not be prepared for the future God has for you.

It can be difficult for us to leave behind what is comfortable and familiar. Most of us don't like change. But do you really want to keep wasting time where you are, wishing for what used to be? Or do you want to move forward in your walk of faith? If so, stop looking back.

When you're looking at Jesus, you won't stumble or become discouraged or distracted. You will find the energy and example you need to run this race of faith. He will become your sole aim and source.

LOOK TO JESUS

If you are not to look around, look inward, or look back, where should you look? Look up to Jesus.

> *Let us fix our eyes on Jesus, the author and perfecter of our faith, who for the joy set before him endured the cross, scorning its shame, and sat down at the right hand of the throne of God.* (HEBREWS 12:2)

We look up, to Jesus. Putting our focus on Jesus puts everything and everyone else in proper perspective.

When you're looking at Jesus, you won't stumble or become discouraged or distracted. You will find the energy and example you need to run this race of faith. He will become your sole aim and source. He will become your one magnificent obsession. And he is a worthy obsession.

In Hebrews 11, the writer has us look at people who lived by faith and persevered in the face of suffering and persecution. And here, in chapter 12, he takes our faces in his hands and moves us from looking at these human, limited examples to looking at the ultimate example of faith. He lifts our eyes to the one who lived the ultimate, perfect life of faith while on this earth—the one who endured more suffering and more persecution than any of the other examples the author has given us. He says, If you really want to persevere in the life of faith, take a look at these faithful followers of God, but then fix your eyes on Jesus, permanently and completely.

It is good to observe these Old Testament examples of faith, but it is imperative that we fix our eyes on Jesus.

The Source That Completes Our Faith

It is when we look at Jesus that we see the source that completes our faith.

Jesus is described here as the author of our faith. As the author, he is the one who is writing the story of your life of faith. He is the source and origin of your faith story. (Remember, you didn't find him; he found you.) Don't begin to think you can live a life of faith without having your eyes fixed on him. You can't live a life of faith with your eyes fixed on a particular church or a particular person or a particular practice. Jesus is your author and source; you have to fix your eyes on him.

Jesus is also the perfecter of your faith. This means he is not only the source of how you got started; he is also the source of how you will complete this faith race.

The Joy of His Completed Work

As we look to Jesus, we will not only see the source that completes our faith; we will see the joy of his completed work. "For the joy set before him . . ." What was the joy set before him that could bring relief into the pain and agony of enduring the Cross?

As Jesus looked ahead, he saw the *joy of redemption.* His endurance of the Cross meant that he paid the debt for sin and justice was satisfied. It brought him a sense of true joy that he was completing the work he was sent to do, which was to pay the price for your sin and mine. As he endured the Cross, he felt a deep sense of joy that the price was now paid so we could spend eternity with him.

Jesus anticipated the *joy of resurrection.* He had told his followers numerous times that he would die and that he would also rise again. But they could not imagine the death, nor could they fathom his resurrection. But Jesus could. And he knew that the shame of the Cross would end and that the result would be the conquering of death forever!

Even as Jesus anticipated the joy ahead, he endured the shame of sin. Jesus never committed any sin to feel shame about. But he took on your shame and my shame, the shame of everyone who has ever regretted what they have said and done, and who they are to the core.

Imagine the shame. The only thing that could bring a glimmer of joy in the midst of enduring all that shame was resurrection. Jesus would break the power of sin and death forever and offer abundant life in the place of immobilizing shame.

Another joy Jesus looked forward to was the *joy of reunion.* Have you seen coverage on the news of soldiers who are returning from distant military posts? Isn't it fun to watch wives reunite with their husbands, children with their daddies, moms with their sons? We watch, and we can just feel the sense of joy and release, can't we? We feel the relief those soldiers feel to finally be home—the joy of a reunion they had dreamed about on their bunks day after day and night after night.

Now imagine Jesus, who lived in perfect fellowship with the Father from before the foundation of the world. He was sent to earth, taking on human flesh, with work to do. And as Jesus headed toward the Cross, doing the work he was sent to do in the magnificent plan of God, Jesus began to anticipate the joy before him. Jesus anticipated the joy of reunion with the Father.

Can you just imagine the joy? As Jesus returned to heaven, having endured the Cross and completed the work, he would be back in the glory he had known before, reunited with the Father he loves so dearly. Surely that joy of anticipating the coming reunion with his Father inspired Jesus as he faced the Cross.

Jesus also knew there was *joy in rest* ahead for him. Verse 12:2 says that after enduring the Cross, he sat down. His most important work was complete.

There's no joy in sitting down when there is still a major task ahead, because the task is nagging. But Jesus' work to save you and me was complete, and now he could rest.

But he isn't just resting. He is ruling. Jesus could see the *joy of rulership* on the other side of the Cross. Jesus sat down at the right hand of the throne of God—a place of honor and authority and usefulness. He reigns. He's the King. And we know that the day is coming when every knee will bow and every tongue will confess that Jesus is Lord. Rulership was part of the joy set before him that enabled him to endure the Cross.

But Jesus is not content to keep this joy to himself! His greatest joy is to share his joy with us—as we are redeemed, as we anticipate a "better resurrection" through which we will be reunited with him and with the Father. We will join him in a place of rest, where we will rule and reign with him forever. What joy!

Why would we look anywhere else than at Jesus as we face the future? Look up to Jesus to see the source that completes your faith and the joy of his finished work.

Consider Him

We can't just look at Jesus and then move on; we have to stop and "consider him."

> *Consider him who endured such opposition from sinful men, so that you will not grow weary and lose heart. In your struggle against sin, you have not yet resisted to the point of shedding your blood. And you have forgotten that word of encouragement that addresses you as sons.* (HEBREWS 12:3-5)

We are not strangers or outsiders; we are God's children. We are welcomed and forgiven so we can boldly approach the throne of God. We can come and linger. As we linger and consider him, we'll find what we need to keep persevering when things get hard so that we won't grow weary and lose heart.

When you feel sorry for yourself because your life is hard . . . consider him. Consider the difficulty of his life of poverty and rejection, and do not lose heart.

When you feel forgotten by God and by those whom you thought cared about you . . . consider him. Consider what it was like for him to be rejected and ridiculed by his own family and hometown. Consider what it must have been like in those moments on the cross when even his Father turned away and he felt forsaken. Consider him, and do not lose heart.

We are God's children. We are welcomed and forgiven so we can boldly approach the throne of God. So we can come and linger.

When you feel tired and you want to give up . . . consider him. Consider how he spent a whole night in prayer, sweating drops of blood, only to endure trials and torture the next day after a night of no sleep. Consider him, and do not grow weary.

When you feel abused and you want to fight back . . . consider him. Consider his humble responses to those who lied about him and spit on him and beat him. Consider him, and do not grow weary.

When you feel fearful about the future . . . consider him, who for the joy set before him endured the Cross, and think of the joy he wants to share with you as you persevere.

Whenever you are tempted to stop running this race of faith, look to the Cross, see the price he paid so that he might call you his very own, and don't let anything hold you back from drawing near.

Consider his love for you; he loves you so much, he will not leave you as you are. He so wants you to run this race of faith well that he is willing to discipline you so that you can finish the race.

SUBMIT TO THE DISCIPLINE OF YOUR FATHER

You have forgotten that word of encouragement that addresses you as sons: "My son, do not make light of the Lord's discipline, and do not lose heart when he rebukes you, because the Lord disciplines those he loves, and he punishes everyone he accepts as a son." . . . If you are not disciplined (and everyone undergoes discipline), then you are illegitimate children and not true sons. (HEBREWS 12:5-6, 8)

God is not mad at you; he does not want to hurt you. But he is willing for you to hurt a little if it will equip you to finish your race well.

Most of us don't want to be disciplined. We want to live life as we please, so we resist God's discipline. The word *discipline* rubs us the wrong way anyway. When we hear *discipline,* we think about work and self-denial and maybe even punishment. Many of us have experienced punishment that was not delivered out of love but out of anger, perhaps even abuse, so we recoil from the very idea.

But God's discipline flows out of his love, not anger. God is not mad at you; he does not want to hurt you. But he is willing for you to hurt a little if it will equip you to finish your race well. God disciplines you as his child—so you have to submit.

If we think about it, we realize that a parent who does not discipline his or her child at all is, in fact, doing that child great harm. An undisciplined child is an unloved child and a miserable child. Children quickly realize that a parent who always lets them have their own way doesn't really care for them.

And we know that while discipline is not pleasant when we experience it, it makes life better in the long run if we learn from it.

One of the favorite stories in my family is about the time when I was about two or three and my sister was four or five and we were both in the back of the station wagon. My dad had threatened my sister a couple of times that if she didn't stop whatever she was doing, he was going to pull over and give her a spanking. Sure enough, she didn't stop. He put on the brakes and came around and opened the back of the car and grabbed for my sister to pull her out and spank her. But instead of grabbing her, he grabbed me by mistake! I was sound asleep in the back of the car and was awakened to a spanking.

Fortunately, God never makes those kinds of mistakes! What we have to understand is that God is the perfect parent. His discipline is never too harsh or inappropriate. Just as a child might think that going to bed with no supper is not fair or that grounding would be better than a spanking, we do not always know what the right discipline for us is. But God does. He is the perfect parent, and he always does what is right.

God Disciplines through Hardship

Endure hardship as discipline; God is treating you as sons. (Hebrews 12:7)

God takes no pleasure in the pain of discipline. In fact, he suffers when we suffer, like the parent who says, "This is going to hurt me more than it hurts you." His discipline is not about punishing us for our sins, though that is often our first thought when suffering comes, isn't it?

I remember waking up the morning after we were given Hope's diagnosis and thinking to myself, *This is my fault. I didn't pray enough for a healthy baby, and now God is making me pay for it.* This is the kind of instinctual indictment that we have to test with Scripture. That was the only way I could overcome the burden of thinking Hope's condition was my fault.

Hardship will either distract our focus from Christ or intensify our focus on him.

How was I able to come to terms with this bitter feeling? By thinking through scriptural examples of how God works with his people and scriptural teaching on the causes of pain and difficulty.

How do we know that our suffering is not punishment for our sin? Because someone has already been punished for our sin. Isaiah 53:5 says, "He was pierced for our transgressions, he was crushed for our iniquities; the punishment that brought us peace was upon him." There is punishment for sin, but that punishment has been laid on Jesus. And when we accept the gift of his sacrifice for our sin, we no longer have to fear being punished for our sin even though we may still experience some of sin's natural consequences.

So would you stop fighting against him and resenting him, and start submitting to him so he can show you his love by disciplining you where you really need it?

God disciplines us through hardship—so we have to endure it. Our suffering is not punishment sent from God, but as we trust God in the midst of it, he can use it as a tool for discipline. Hardship will either distract our focus from Christ or intensify our focus on him. If we give in to grumbling and complaining about the hardships and difficulties in our lives, we will miss out on what there is to learn from them. But if we allow our difficulties to intensify our focus on Jesus and intensify our determination to persevere, God's discipline will have its desired effect, and God's purposes in the hardship will be fulfilled.

IF SUFFERING ISN'T PUNISHMENT, WHAT IS IT?

Some suffering is the natural consequence of our sinful choices and the sinful choices of others.
Proverbs 22:8 says, "He who sows wickedness reaps trouble," and Paul told the Galatians the same thing: "Do not be deceived: God cannot be mocked. A man reaps what he sows. The one who sows to please his sinful nature, from that nature will reap destruction" (6:7-8).

God does not always prevent the natural consequences of sinful choices from taking a toll on our lives. The natural consequence of abusing alcohol might be liver disease or the loss of a job. The natural consequence of pride and self-centeredness is often broken relationships with those we care about. And sometimes our suffering is the natural consequence of someone else's sin: A parent feeds his perverted passions, so a child suffers as a victim of sexual abuse; a driver is drunk and swerves on the road, so innocent people in another car are killed.

Some suffering is the natural result of living in a fallen, broken world.
The book of Romans helps us understand that "when Adam sinned, sin entered the world. Adam's sin brought death, so death spread to everyone, for everyone sinned" (5:12, NLT). Romans 8 says, "Against its will, all creation was subjected to God's curse" (verse 20, NLT).

This world is broken, and we regularly experience this brokenness in the form of suffering. Death, disease, destruction—these are all the result of living in a world where sin has taken root and corrupted everything. So many people are quick to blame God when something bad happens. But it is not God who deserves the blame. It's sin. So rather than saying, "I'm so mad at God!" when the pain of this broken world hurts us, we should say, "I'm so mad at sin! I'm so angry about the cruel effects of sin on this world!"

Some suffering is the supernatural work of Satan.
According to 1 Peter 5:8, Satan "prowls around like a roaring lion looking for someone to devour." How does he "devour" us? Satan brings suffering into our lives in an effort to destroy our faith.

That is certainly what we see in the story of Job, when we read that Satan was responsible for afflicting Job. We see it also in 2 Corinthians 12:7, where Paul describes a thorn in his flesh as being a "messenger of Satan" sent to torment him.

Our consoling confidence as believers is that our suffering, whether brought on by our sin, the fallenness of the world, or Satan himself—from the greatest catastrophes to the smallest annoyances—is all guided by the merciful providence of God (see Job 1–2; Acts 2:22-23; 4:27-28). What Satan means to hurt us can, in God's hands, become a tool of discipline, used for good in our lives.

God Disciplines for Our Good

> *God disciplines us for our good, that we may share in his holiness.* (HEBREWS 12:10)

When you truly believe that your Father loves you, you can accept that God disciplines you for your good—so you can share in his holiness.

When God allows hardship into our lives, believe it or not, it is for our good. The hardship itself might not be what we would describe as a good thing, but when we are his children, we can be confident that God will use it for a good purpose. And his purpose is always the same: to mold us into people who look and think and act like Jesus. He wants us to share in the holiness of Jesus. That is the grand aim of God's discipline: to make us holy and happy like Jesus.

That is the grand aim of God's discipline: to make us holy and happy like Jesus.

I don't mean for you to take offense, but becoming like Jesus is going to require some discipline that may make you uncomfortable. And you're not going to make any progress toward holiness without it. It is good for you to learn that sin hurts you, so God might allow you to experience the pain that is the natural consequence of your sinful choices. It is good for you to learn that disobedience leads to emptiness and regret, so he might allow you to feel the pain of that regret.

When we make the sinful choice to gossip, we find ourselves experiencing the pain of broken relationships—the natural consequence of our sinful choice. When we give our bodies away to lovers other than our spouses and discover that the brief pleasure was not worth the ripple effect of our unfaithfulness, God allows us to feel the pain of our regret.

The greater our disobedience, the heavier the discipline we need. And the flip side is that the most holy of us are those who have endured the most discipline—those who have not disregarded it or become indifferent to it but have heeded it.

God Disciplines Us for Training

Finally, God disciplines us for training—so our lives will produce righteousness and peace.

> *No discipline seems pleasant at the time, but painful. Later on, however, it produces a harvest of righteousness and peace for those who have been trained by it.* (HEBREWS 12:11)

The purpose of God's discipline is not to hurt us or make us feel worthless—it is purposeful, and the purpose is to help us grow and mature. Learning from God's discipline is no fun at the time, but when we are willing to be trained by it—to be molded and shaped by it—it results in God's richest, most rewarding blessings: righteousness and peace. An abundance of peace and joy that come from knowing everything is right between us and God. This kind of peace and joy comes from allowing God's discipline to rub off our rough edges so that instead of producing discord and disobedience, we produce righteousness and peace.

I can't help but think of the *Peanuts* character Pig-Pen. Do you remember how he would walk around with a cloud of dust and dirt following him wherever he went? Some of us seem to kick up a cloud of misunderstandings and harsh words and hurt feelings everywhere we go. It is always following us. But this is not what follows the woman who is allowing herself to be trained by the discipline of God. She leaves behind the sweet fragrance of peaceful and profitable relationships. She leaves people feeling blessed by her presence, not broken by it.

Would you submit to God's discipline and be trained by it so that you might begin to experience a growing holiness in your character, rightness in your living, and peacefulness in your countenance?

Would you submit to God's discipline and be trained by it so that you might begin to experience a growing holiness in your character, rightness in your living, and peacefulness in your countenance?

All of us are racing toward something. Some of us are headed down dead-end roads. Some of us are going in circles. Some of us are running toward many other obsessions in our aimlessness. But can you see that Jesus is the only obsession worth running toward and giving ourselves to? Won't you run toward him and draw near to him?

As we cut away the sin that is tripping us up and whatever is weighing us down, we'll be set free to run with a lightness to our step. We'll see progress toward the heart of God—progress that we've never known but have always wanted.

We have to stop looking around at others, inward at ourselves, or back at the past so we can look up and see Jesus in all his fullness and sufficiency. But when we do, we'll see the source of our completed faith and the joy of his completed work, and we'll experience that joy along with him now and forevermore.

We also have to stop resisting God's discipline so that we can receive the endurance and holiness and peace that our loving Father has for us.

Fix your eyes on Jesus, and don't let anything hold you back from drawing near to him.

Jesus is the energy behind and the ultimate destination of our faith race.

CHAPTER 10

what are you dreaming of?

HEBREWS 12:25-13:25

ABOUT EIGHT YEARS AGO I was on my way to Colorado Springs for a business conference. My friends Dan and Sue Johnson were going to the same conference and were on my flight. I rode with them to the hotel, and on that little trip we had a very meaningful and memorable conversation.

For some reason we were talking about our dreams—not the dreams we have when we're asleep, but the dreams we nurture deep inside. And that day I dared to share with them the dream inside me that I had not shared with anyone up to that point. Honestly I was embarrassed to say it out loud because I felt it was too lofty and unrealistic, too far from a possibility. It was as if saying it out loud might completely crush it.

For six years I had been attending the Bible study class that Sue taught on a weekly basis, and each week it was as if the lesson was just for me. It challenged me and changed me, and as I looked around I saw other women being changed through the power of the Word too. That day in Colorado I told Dan

Are your dreams molded by the culture we live in and what this world values and recognizes? Or have your dreams been shaped and reborn as the Holy Spirit remakes you and as the Word of God renews your mind?

and Sue that I couldn't imagine doing anything more significant with my life than doing what Sue was doing—I told them that I had a dream to teach the Bible. But honestly I couldn't imagine that I would ever have the understanding or the ability or the credibility to do it.

And while the route God has taken me on in bringing this dream to reality is not what I expected or necessarily would have wanted, when I get to stand up in front of a group of people and open up the Scriptures, it is so much fun and so fulfilling to me, I almost have to pinch myself.

I tell you about this dream because I want to get you thinking about what *your* dreams are. I wonder what you want out of this life, what you want to accomplish, who you want to become. I wonder what dreams of yours seem lofty and unrealistic and unreachable. And I wonder if so far you have settled for small dreams—dreams that are earthbound and self-centered and simpleminded, dreams that settle for the best this world has to offer—rather than the ones that reach beyond for something more solid and more significant.

Are your dreams molded by the culture we live in and what this world values and recognizes? Or have your dreams been shaped and reborn as the Holy Spirit remakes you and as the Word of God renews your mind?

The end of Hebrews 12 through Hebrews 13 helps us to see what defines a worthwhile dream for a significant and satisfying life. This passage reveals to us what a life that is worth longing for and dreaming of and working toward really is. And if we will allow these truths to instruct us, we can trade in our earthbound, small-minded, self-centered dreams for bigger, more satisfying, more significant dreams—dreams that have been born in the heart of God and are designed for each of us individually.

A SECURE LIFE

A life worthy of the investment of our dreams and desires is a secure life. But first we have to look at what causes a life to be shaken or insecure.

See to it that you do not refuse him who speaks. If they did not escape when they refused him who warned them on earth, how much less will we, if we turn away from him who warns us from heaven? At that time his voice shook the earth, but now he has promised, "Once more I will shake not only the earth but also the heavens." The words "once more" indicate the removing of what can be shaken—that is, created things—so that what cannot be shaken may remain. Therefore, since we are receiving a kingdom that cannot be shaken, let us be thankful, and so worship God acceptably with reverence and awe, for our "God is a consuming fire." (HEBREWS 12:25-29)

A Kingdom That Can't Be Shaken

Verse 26 says, "At that time his voice shook the earth." What time was this? When God spoke on Mount Sinai, revealing himself in the Law. Exodus 19:18 records the event: "Mount Sinai was covered with smoke, because the LORD descended on it in fire. The smoke billowed up from it like smoke from a furnace, the whole mountain trembled violently." God was literally laying down the Law, and the force of it shook the earth.

As Jesus cried out from the cross, the earth shook again: "When Jesus had cried out again in a loud voice, he gave up his spirit. At that moment the curtain of the temple was torn in two from top to bottom. The earth shook and the rocks split" (Matthew 27:50-51). Why did the earth shake? Because the judgment of God was falling to punish sin. The judgment you and I deserve for the things we've said and done and for our rejection of God fell on Jesus that day. And the force of the tremendous weight of that judgment shook the earth.

"Once more" in verse 26 refers to a shaking in the future. This is the violent shaking of creation prophesied in numerous Old Testament and New Testament passages, including Revelation 6:12, 15-17:

I watched as he opened the sixth seal. There was a great earthquake. . . . Then the kings of the earth, the princes, the generals, the rich, the mighty, and every slave and every free man hid in caves and among the rocks of the mountains. They called to the mountains and the rocks, "Fall on us and hide us from the face of him who sits on the throne and from the wrath of the Lamb! For the great day of their wrath has come, and who can stand?"

The day is coming when once again the judgment of God will shake the earth. How can we escape this terrifying shaking of the earth? How can we have a secure life, an unshakable life, knowing that this future shaking of the earth at the final judgment of God is sure and certain?

The secret is in verse 25. It seems to take us back to where we started in Hebrews. Remember Hebrews 1:1-2? "In the past God spoke to our forefathers through the prophets at many times and in various ways, but in these last days he has spoken to us by his Son." Now in verse 25 of chapter 12, he offers us this final major warning: "See to it that you do not refuse him who speaks."

> Jesus is worthy of becoming our better obsession. And now he is awakening us to a better way of life than our old dreams caused us to long for.

God speaks to us through the person and work of Jesus. The writer of Hebrews has been opening our eyes to the beauty and majesty and sufficiency and superiority of this final Word, Jesus, telling us that Jesus is better. He's better than angels, better than Moses. He offers a better rest. He's a better priest of a better covenant in a better sanctuary, having offered himself as a better sacrifice. He has opened up his home to us so that we might long for a better homeland. He is worthy of becoming our better obsession. And now he is awakening us to a better way of life than our old dreams caused us to long for.

God has been speaking to you personally through the book of Hebrews, showing himself to you, offering himself to you, inviting you to draw near. Oh, my friend, see to it that you do not refuse him who speaks. He holds out to you the life you've dreamed of—a secure life—the security of knowing that you are safe in his care for eternity.

A Firm Foundation

Of course, a secure life doesn't mean that our lives in this world will never be rocked by difficulty. Many of us know what it is for our lives to be affected by pain or disappointment or disaster.

That day in the car with Dan and Sue, I shared with them a second secret dream. I told them that David and I wanted to have another child. What I didn't know that day was that I was already pregnant. But never could I have imagined how that baby girl and her little brother would rock my world. Neither could I have imagined that the death of this dream would become the birthplace for my dream to teach.

Often when I do radio or TV interviews about our experiences with loving and losing Hope and Gabriel, interviewers ask me, "How did you do it? How did you keep your faith in the face of such tremendous loss?" And the only way I know how to answer that question is by telling the story Jesus told in Luke 6:47-49 about the wise man and the foolish man. Jesus said, "I will show you what he is like who comes to me and hears my words and puts them into practice. He is like a man building a house, who dug down deep and laid the foundation on rock. When a flood came, the torrent struck that house but could not shake it, because it was well built. But the one who hears my words and does not put them into practice is like a man who built a house on the ground without a foundation. The moment the torrent struck that house, it collapsed and its destruction was complete."

Did you notice the difference between the two men? Both of them heard God's Word, and both of them were struck by the storm. The difference was that the wise man not only heard the Word, he put it into practice. He worked these words into his life.

All those mornings I spent in the front row while Sue gave out God's Word—as I wrestled with the implications of what I was learning, and as I repented and allowed God to change me—I was hearing God's Word and putting it into practice. I was working those words into my life. And so, when sorrow rained down on my life, I wasn't destroyed by it.

It wasn't that I'm a strong person or that I have great faith. It was because of the firm foundation underneath me, the foundation of knowing God by studying his Word. It was the Rock of Ages undergirding my life, providing for me a secure, unshakable foundation so that when the storm hit, it didn't crush me.

It is so easy for us to build our lives on unstable foundations. They look good, but they are not secure. For many of us, our life dreams are secured by a job or a husband or our savings or our health or our position. But if these are the building blocks we're depending on, our lives are not secure, because all these things and people are vulnerable to being shaken.

> Jesus himself offers you the secure life you've dreamed of now and for eternity.

Jesus himself offers you the secure life you've dreamed of now and for eternity. And as you work his words into your life, you will discover that no matter what happens to you or around you, no matter what rocks your world, you will not be shaken. Your life will be secure.

A PASSIONATE LIFE

For some, a secure life could sound like a boring life, a risk-free life, a passionless life. But that is not at all what God wants us to dream of. He made us to be people of passion. Who among us did not grow up dreaming of a passionate romance?

Remember writing on your notebook in junior high? Nancy + David = Love Forever. Then you wrote out your first name with his last name just to see how it looked. Do you remember the first movie you saw that awakened deep longing for a passionate romance? Mine was *Love Story,* the tragic, intense story of two lovers who believed that "love is never having to say you're sorry." Oh, brother!

God doesn't want us to let go of the dreams he gave us for a life of passion. But out of love for us, he does want us to carefully guard and channel our passions.

A Passion for People

> *Keep on loving each other as brothers. Do not forget to entertain strangers, for by so doing some people have entertained angels without knowing it. Remember those in prison as if you were their fellow prisoners, and those who are mistreated as if you yourselves were suffering.* (HEBREWS 13:1-3)

First, God wants us to channel our passions toward other people. "Keep on loving each other as brothers [and sisters]." How would you describe your love for your brother or sister? When you were a kid, while you might have tried to come up with the most evil, ugly put-down name you could think of to call your brothers and sisters, when someone else criticized or threatened your siblings, remember how you came to their defense? Loving each other as brother or sister is a protective love.

And it is an accepting love. After spending all those years growing up with the brothers and sisters God gave us, no matter how annoying some of their qualities may be, we just accept them. By now we know that that is just the way they are, the way they've always been. Love helps us overlook what offends.

Loving each other as brothers and sisters is also a defining love. It is not casual or superficial. It is not temporary or trite. There is a depth of affection and commitment that defines who we are by whom we're related to. This is how God calls us to love our brothers and sisters in Christ. This is not passive. It is passionate and at times costly.

I'll never forget that difficult day when we put Gabe's body in the ground, what it was like to look up and see my sisters—my fellow Bible Study Fellowship leaders—walking up the hill toward the grave. It took my breath away, as well as my fragile composure for the task at hand. They had been there with me all the way, and there they were to be at my side on that hard day, too. Then I looked around and saw close friends from college days and many others who had been so faithful to us through Gabe's life and now at his death. Why? Because they loved Gabe and they loved us with such a defining love, there was nowhere else they would have chosen to be. Oh, how good it felt to be loved by my brothers and sisters in Christ on that bitterly cold and enormously sorrowful day.

But we are not just to love those close to us; we are also to "entertain strangers." We are to extend ourselves to those who are different from us and unfamiliar to us. They may look strange or smell strange or dress strangely or eat strange foods or speak a strange language or have strange ideas. And we are called not just to tolerate them but to reach out to them. Invite them into our homes. Accept them into the body of Christ. We are to become passionate about turning strangers into friends.

Next, we are to channel our passions toward those suffering in prison. The secret for generating that passion, according to this passage, is to think about what it would be like—what we would want and need—if we were the ones suffering or in prison. What difference would it make in our willingness to minister to those in prison if we thought about what it would feel like to be imprisoned? What difference would it make in the way we regarded the mistreated if we thought about what it would feel like to be mistreated in the same way? Would it turn up our passion flame? Caring for those in prisons of concrete as well as prisons of addiction and abuse and poverty and pain requires that our passion move beyond our own needs and concerns—that we become passionate about the needs and hurts of others.

A Passion for Purity

Marriage should be honored by all, and the marriage bed kept pure, for God will judge the adulterer and all the sexually immoral. (HEBREWS 13:4)

In addition to a passion for people, God wants to channel our sexual passions into purity. "Marriage should be honored by all, and the marriage bed kept pure." Notice that God does not say to us women who long for a grand romance, "You shouldn't want that so much." Nor does he say, "Christian women shouldn't enjoy sexual pleasure." He says that marriage should be honored and respected. God is no prude when it comes to sex, and he doesn't expect you to be either. Sex was God's good idea, a gift he has given to us out of his love for our enjoyment, as a means of building an intimate bond between us and our husbands, as a comfort, as a way to grow our families.

The reason God wants us to keep the marriage bed pure is that he knows how it breaks our hearts and crushes our dreams when we try to fulfill our desires for passion and romance in any other way than within marriage. His design for marriage is that it give us a taste of the satisfaction we will experience when we give ourselves completely to him. The passion of sex helps us to grasp the passion he wants us to enjoy with him as we draw near, and the ultimate passionate oneness we will experience when we are one day in his presence.

A Passion for Contentment

Keep your lives free from the love of money and be content with what you have. (HEBREWS 13:5)

The third kind of passion God wants to give us, according to this passage, is a passion for contentment. Most of us are not naturally content. Even though we have so much more than most other people on the face of the earth, we're still not content. We want new outfits, new cars, new houses, new bodies. Sometimes I catch myself wanting something I own to break so I'll have a good excuse for buying a new one! What is this thrill we derive from plunking down our cash or plastic to get more?

> The life of your dreams is not purchased by money, and it is not found in the constant pursuit of one more thing. That is a life of tyranny and dissatisfaction. The life of your dreams is found in learning to be content.

Money is not a neutral thing. It has power. It has the power to steal away our passion. It has the power to make us do and say things we would never want to do or say. How often are we willing to compromise our integrity for just a few bucks? How often are we willing to sacrifice our witness to drive a better bargain? How many times have we been in relationships that have gone sour over money?

The life of your dreams is not purchased by money, and it is not found in the constant pursuit of one more thing. That is a life of tyranny and dissatisfaction. The life of your dreams is found in learning to be content.

We think we'll be content when we finally get what we want, but real contentment is found when we accept something less than what we want or something other than what we want. That is real freedom. And it doesn't just happen, because this world is telling us, "You deserve it; you've earned it; it is waiting for you." You have to pursue contentment with an unrelenting passion. Just imagine how deeply satisfying a life of being content with what you have could be—a life of confidence in God rather than confidence in money and what it will buy.

A SACRIFICIAL LIFE

A secure life and a passionate life sound good to us. While we might have pursued them in the wrong way, they at least seem compatible with the dreams we've had for our lives. But from there the writer to the Hebrews turns our dreams upside down. He begins to show us a better way to live, a better dream to pursue. It is a life of sacrifice.

A Sacrifice of Acceptance

> *Jesus also suffered outside the city gate to make the people holy through his own blood. Let us, then, go to him outside the camp, bearing the disgrace he bore. For here we do not have an enduring city, but we are looking for the city that is to come.* (HEBREWS 13:12-14)

The sacrificial life described here is not necessarily the life we've been dreaming of on our own. We were hoping to turn heads with our beauty and brilliance, and instead the author to the Hebrews is telling us that real satisfaction is found in sharing the disgrace of Jesus on the cross—like a common criminal on the outskirts of town. We've dreamed of acceptance, and he is calling us to a life of being rejected because of our identification with Christ. He is calling us to the life of an outsider when we so love the power and thrills that come with being on the inside track. While we thought that our dreams would come true by being applauded and lauded by the crowd, he calls us to share not the applause but the reproach of Jesus.

We are asked to trade in acceptance in the here and now, the city of this world, for the welcome we will receive in the next life, the city to come. When we walk into that city, nothing we have sacrificed will seem like a sacrifice. It will have been worth it. Jesus will be worth it. He will be worth leaving behind everything we walk away from so that we can draw near to him outside the camp—outside the boundaries of acceptance drawn by this world.

A Sacrifice of Praise

> *Through Jesus, therefore, let us continually offer to God a sacrifice of praise—the fruit of lips that confess his name.* (HEBREWS 13:15)

Not only does the life of our dreams demand that we sacrifice acceptance, it demands a sacrifice of praise. Have you determined that Jesus is worthy of praise that costs you something? Or are you willing to give only the praise that is comfortable for you to give? What would make your praise a sacrifice? Praise becomes sacrificial when it is one step closer to what Jesus deserves and one step out of your comfort zone.

Is raising your hands in praise to God one step out of your comfort zone? Perhaps that is the step of sacrifice for you. Is it physically getting on your knees when you pray? Is it lying prostrate on the ground and crying out to him with tears? Would the place you offer praise to God—or the people you're with—make it a sacrifice? Would it be a sacrifice of praise to speak of your love for Jesus at the club or around the table with your family at Christmas dinner?

Praise becomes sacrificial when it is one step closer to what Jesus deserves and one step out of your comfort zone.

When we choose to praise God for his goodness, despite his allowing what we would not describe as good into our lives, that is a sacrifice of praise. When we praise him for his sovereignty, even though we don't understand the whys of his plans, that is a sacrifice of praise.

Would you be willing this week or even today to offer Jesus a sacrifice of praise?

A Sacrifice of Sharing

> *Do not forget to do good and to share with others, for with such sacrifices God is pleased.* (HEBREWS 13:16)

While our dreams usually consist of collecting things, this passage tells us that the life of our dreams is better defined by sharing things. Remember when you were small and you were always told to share your toys? Well, how are you doing with sharing your stuff now? I'm not talking about giving away what you don't want or can't use anymore. When was the last time you gave away something that was valuable and usable to you for the sheer joy of it? Do you need a reminder about learning to share?

"For with such sacrifices God is pleased." Ahhh. That is what we're going for; that is what we're dreaming of. That is what makes a sacrificial life the life of our dreams: It is pleasing to God. And the closer we draw to him, the more we find that what pleases him pleases us.

The closer we draw to him, the more we find that what pleases him pleases us.

But why is sacrifice on our part pleasing to God? Is he

needy, or does it feed his ego? No—he asks us to sacrifice not because he needs it but because we need to offer it.

I started working in my dad's drugstore as soon as I could stand on a box and reach the cash register. The first big thing I bought with the money I had earned was a bicycle. I took good care of that bicycle because I had worked so hard for it—probably better than I would have if it had been given to me. It's just human nature that we value what we sacrifice for.

Our willingness to sacrifice in pursuit of God reflects just how precious he is to us. And likewise, if he is not precious to us, perhaps it is because we have never sacrificed anything for him. While we may give lip service to drawing nearer to God, our willingness to sacrifice for it reveals whether or not our desire is genuine.

A SUBMISSIVE LIFE

When I was in college I read the book *Improving Your Serve*, by Charles Swindoll, and it impacted me deeply. I remember hearing him say once, "No one ever says, 'When I grow up I want to be a servant.'" Most of us don't see servanthood as part of our dream-life package. But if we do not nurture this dream in our lives, we will always be miserable. It is the dream of a submissive life.

Submission to Authority

> *Obey your leaders and submit to their authority. They keep watch over you as men who must give an account. Obey them so that their work will be a joy, not a burden, for that would be of no advantage to you. Pray for us. We are sure that we have a clear conscience and desire to live honorably in every way.* (Hebrews 13:17-18)

So often the word *submit* just rubs us the wrong way, doesn't it? We're always looking for the loophole and bringing up the "yes, but" when it comes to submission. We've seen authority abused, so there is a part of us that agrees with the bumper sticker that says, Question Authority. Frankly, we're suspicious of authority. Our automatic reflex to authority is usually not submission.

So when we read, "Obey your leaders and submit to their authority," we chafe a bit at the suggestion. We're a little too sophisticated for that. In the world of our dreams, we are in charge—or at least we're free to do as we please. Our dreams do not include much obedience or submission. And yet because God loves us and knows what we need to lead the life we've always dreamed of, he tells us that submission to godly leaders is what will make us truly happy and holy.

Could it be that submitting to not getting your own way would create the spiritual breakthrough you've been longing for? Could it be that God has ordained a leader over you to challenge you in ways that make you uncomfortable, to prod you toward growth? Is God calling you to trust him in more significant ways than you have in the past by submitting to the authority of the leaders he has placed over you—not because you think they are right but because you trust God?

Could it be that submitting to not getting your own way would create the spiritual breakthrough you've been longing for?

Forgive me for taking this a step closer to home, but I've got to ask. Do you approach your service to your church with the mind-set of a volunteer who needs to be appreciated and cannot be criticized, or as a servant who respects authority and is willing to be held accountable for what you do and how you do it?

Sunday school teachers, if the children's ministry director in your church asks you to administer discipline in a different way in your class, will you just get mad and quit, or will you submit? Small group leaders, if your leader asks you to use your group time in a different way, will you respond in submission or resent the intrusion, thinking, *If they don't like the way I do it then just forget it!*

In order to honor a leader we don't naturally respect and submit to authority we disagree with, we will need the Holy Spirit to work in us to make us humble and flexible and submissive!

Submission to Scrutiny

Did you notice that this passage does not indicate that your leaders are accountable to you? It is God who holds leaders accountable for the way they live and lead. Verse 7 says, "Remember your leaders, who spoke the word of God to you. Consider the outcome of their way of life and imitate their faith." If you are a leader, people have a right to hold you to a higher standard. They have the right to examine whether or not you practice what you preach, whether or not you lead a life that is worthy of imitation. These are the things God expects of you.

This is what scared me most about my dream to teach the Bible and what made this dream seem out of reach—I'm so aware of my own weaknesses and inconsistencies. I realize that those I teach and lead are right to expect me to live in a way that is consistent with what I say. And God expects that of me. So I just had to decide: Do I want to be held to that higher standard, or do I want to keep my options open for living as I please? Do I want to be accountable and therefore discipline myself, or do I want my freedom so that no one (including myself) expects too much from me?

I teach and write not because I am perfect or because I pursue God perfectly but because I want to pursue him passionately. He is replacing my dreams of living for myself with a new dream of living as a woman under authority, a woman who is willing to step up and lead but likewise willing to submit to accountability. And that is the dream that I believe will make me truly happy. It is the dream I want to give myself to.

Are you holding back from stepping up to lead because you resist not only serving under authority but also serving under scrutiny? Do you resist accountability and transparency? What sin are you protecting? Are there things you want to keep hidden that would have to be done away with if you stepped forward to lead? Don't you want to get rid of whatever it is that you know is displeasing to God, no matter what? And if stepping up to lead is the accountability and push you need to get rid of the thing that holds you back, isn't that what you really want?

THE PLEASING LIFE

There was something I learned in the Bible study I was in that ultimately gave me the courage to embrace my dream to teach the Bible. It is the truth that God equips us for whatever he calls us to. We see it here in verses 20-21:

> *May the God of peace, who through the blood of the eternal covenant brought back from the dead our Lord Jesus, that great Shepherd of the sheep, equip you with everything good for doing his will, and may he work in us what is pleasing to him, through Jesus Christ, to whom be glory for ever and ever. Amen.*

You see, God wants to replace our selfish dream of pleasing ourselves with the more satisfying dream of pleasing him. He wants us to set our affections toward a life that is pleasing to him.

Cleansed and Covered

But we just can't do this on our own. In fact, we can never be good enough to be pleasing to God. Do you see what this verse says about how we please God? It is through the blood of Christ. We try so hard to be pleasing on our own. But we need to give it up! We can't do it! We have to let that pipe dream die. Instead, we need to be filled with the longing to be pleasing to God—not through our own beauty or perfection or work or sacrifice, but through the sacrifice of Jesus, the blood of Jesus.

Called and Equipped

We also need to trust God to equip us with "everything good for doing his will" and to work in us "what is pleasing to him, through Jesus Christ." Do you have a dream that you are wondering about right now—wondering if it is born out of your flesh or implanted in you by the Spirit of God? I do. I have another big one—once again too big, too lofty for my current abilities and understanding. I'm still trying to figure out if this is a dream from God or one born of my own ambition. Sometimes it is hard for me to tell, so I have to move slowly and prayerfully and humbly.

We're right to question carefully the origin of our dreams. We are right to test them carefully. Because sometimes it is hard to tell where our own ambition ends and God's dream begins. But here is how we know, I think: When they are our ambitions, we find ourselves trying to push open doors for ourselves. When the dream is from God, we plan and prepare but we don't push. When our dream is motivated by our own ambition, we want to measure success by how much, how many, how often. But the work of the Spirit is not measurable in those terms. If the dream is from God, we're content to wait on his timing, accept his way of doing it, and accept the results he brings about. We don't make demands. We're not pushing

If the dream is from God, we're content to wait on his timing, accept his way of doing it, and accept the results he brings about.

an agenda. We're not seeking to be somebody. We just want to be usable to God. We want to be ordinary vessels of clay that he can use for whatever purpose he has in mind—impressive or ordinary, visible or behind the scenes, big or small. That is the fulfillment of our dreams—to be used by God to build his Kingdom. That is the ultimate thrill of life—a dream worthy of all of our energies and emotion. Jesus replaces our small-minded, self-centered, earthbound dreams with dreams that are worth our pursuit.

When a dream is from God, our heads do not swell with pride in our accomplishment because we are fully aware of where our abilities and opportunities come from. We realize that God has been faithful to "equip [us] with everything good for doing his will." He gives us the abilities, the opportunities—everything we need. He opens doors for us so that we can walk through them with the confidence that he is in it, he has done it, and he will do it.

So what are you dreaming of? Is it a dream that is worthy of your energy and investment? Is it a dream that will help you to draw near, or will it take you away from or distract you from Christ? If it is from God, I guarantee you it will move you closer to Christ and make you more dependent on Christ's power, because that is what he wants. That is what he has been telling us over and over throughout Hebrews. Have you heard that call? Have you responded to that call?

See to it that you do not refuse him who speaks.

Don't refuse his kindness; don't refuse his grace; don't refuse his help in time of need; don't refuse his holiness; don't refuse his love. Open yourself to it. Receive it. Celebrate it.

Nourish the dream he has placed inside you for something better—a life of security, passion, sacrifice, and submission—a life that is pleasing to him.

Jesus replaces our small-minded, self-centered, earthbound dreams with dreams that are worth our pursuit.

are you ready for something better?

We started this study with three goals, adopting for ourselves the same goals as the writer to the Hebrews had:

GOAL #1: TO GO DEEPER

Has this happened? Would you say that your eyes have been opened to Jesus in a fresh way? Do you see him a little more clearly; do you hold him in higher estimation? And do you find yourself drawn to him like never before? Can you see that Jesus himself is worthy of your careful and constant consideration and your deepest and most costly devotion? Have you gone deeper?

GOAL #2: TO DRAW CLOSER

Do you find yourself moving in Jesus' direction, wanting to draw closer to him? Do you find yourself more determined than ever to keep pursuing him with every day he chooses to give you in this life?

We have to answer the same question the early Hebrew believers had to answer: Will we keep moving forward with Jesus—no matter what happens, no matter what it costs us—believing that the closer we draw to him the more we enter into something better?

No believer can cope with adversity for following Christ unless she has determined that Christ is "worth it." Have you decided that Jesus is worth it?

Are you so thoroughly convinced of the supreme value of Jesus and the surety of the eternal reward he has promised that you are willing to risk everything for him?

GOAL #3: TO HOLD TIGHTER

Have you figured out what it will mean for you to live as if Jesus is your only hope for a life of rest and joy and meaning—both here and in the hereafter?

I think that perhaps we don't know if we are thoroughly convinced of the superiority and sufficiency and necessity of Jesus until it costs us something. At least, I think that was the case for me.

I have been a publicist in Christian publishing for over twenty years. In that role I've worked with all kinds of media representing a number of Christian authors. And while I think it has always been obvious that I share the beliefs of those I represent, I suppose I've been able to conveniently distance myself a bit at times.

But a few years ago I found myself sitting in a restaurant interview with a journalist who has become a cherished friend, and honestly it was awkward. She was interviewing me for a story that would be on the front page of a major newspaper. And I knew that as I answered her questions, I was not only speaking to her millions of readers but also to her, my friend—my Jewish friend, my devoted-to-her-faith and active-in-her-synagogue Jewish friend. I respect her greatly and didn't want to be offensive. So when she asked me why I felt it was necessary in my book *Holding on to Hope* to say that knowing God was only possible through a relationship with his Son, Jesus, I was uncomfortably aware that I was speaking to her as well as to her readers.

"You know, you could sell a lot more books if you just left that out," she told me. And I knew she was right.

That night in bed, as I thought about what it would be like to have my words about the necessity of Jesus made so public, I told David, "I feel like I have walked out on a plank and I'm getting ready to dive (or be pushed) into the cold waters of criticism." Whereas before in my work with the media it had always been someone else's ideas and views put into print, this time it was my words, my beliefs and opinions, my experiences that would be broadcast and held up to scrutiny. And I found myself wondering, *Do I so believe this to be true that I am willing to be disagreed with and considered intolerant and small-minded?*

And my answer is yes. I believe it is true. I believe Jesus is who he said he is. I believe Jesus is the Lord of the universe, the only Son of God, the only Savior of the world. And I not only believe this with my mind; I've chosen to entrust my life to this Jesus. I want to give him everything. I'm staking everything on who Jesus is and what he has done.

God has invited us to draw near to him, and he has made a way for us to be acceptable to him. And though it may be offensive to many people in this world who hang on to the view that "all faiths are valid," I'm willing to go on record as saying that Scripture teaches salvation through Jesus Christ alone.

Will you walk out on this plank with me and stake your life on the significance and sufficiency and superiority of Jesus?

Perhaps the plank for you is making a first-time commitment to Jesus. Walking out on a plank for you would mean coming to Jesus as you are and telling him that you need him and want him in your life—that you turn from the way you've been living because now you see that his way is better, that he is better.

Perhaps the plank for you requires that you take a step further in your commitment to him—perhaps going public with him, giving up something for him, or letting go of something in this world so that you can grab on to Jesus and never let go. Won't you grab hold of something better? Some*one* better?

Because Jesus is better.

He's really better.

Jesus is the something better we've been hoping for all along.

CHAPTER 1

Take some time to read Hebrews 1:1–2:4 and work your way through the following questions before reading chapter 1.

List at least six things we are told about Jesus in verses 1-4.

1.

2.

3.

4.

5.

6.

Which one of these aspects of who Jesus is do you find especially meaningful, and why?

What do you think it means that "in these last days [God] has spoken to us by his Son" (1:2)?

Some say that Hebrews 1:1-4 expresses the most important idea in history. How would you express this idea in your own words?

What is the common concept of angels today? Compare that view with what the writer says about the duties and position of angels in 1:4-7, 13-14.

What does each of the following passages add to your understanding of the role of angels?

1 Kings 19:5-7

Psalm 34:7

Luke 1:13, 30

Acts 10:3-5

Acts 12:23

Revelation 5:11-12

As you follow the line of argument in 1:5-14, what does the writer intend to prove about Jesus Christ's position in relation to angels?

What responsibilities and authority does the Son have according to 1:8-9?

The writer has shown Jesus as superior in rank and in power to the prophets and to angels. What is Jesus shown to be superior to in 1:10-12?

According to 1:13-14, where is the Son? Where are the angels? How does this add to the superiority of Jesus?

Put into your own words the warning in Hebrews 2:1-4.

How does the culture we live in entice us to drift away from what God has said? What difference does understanding who Jesus is make in our tendency to drift?

Do you see yourself as paying careful attention to Jesus or drifting away? What changes can you make in your life to guard against drifting away? What divine promises can you cling to in fueling these changes?

What was the reason for the signs, wonders, and miracles of Jesus according to verses 2:3-4? (See also John 10:38 and Acts 2:22.)

CHAPTER 2

Take some time to read Hebrews 2:5-18 and work your way through the following questions before reading chapter 2.

What point do you think the writer was trying to make to his readers by quoting Psalm 8 in 2:6-8?

Hebrews 2:5 says God did not intend angels to be in charge of the world to come (when the world is redeemed and returns to its original perfection). According to 2:6-8, who did God make to rule over the earth?

Understanding that Psalm 8 celebrates humanity's original destiny and that it is also a prophetic or messianic psalm, who is the ultimate "son of man" who fulfilled our original destiny?

Hebrews 2:8 says that "we do not see everything subject to him" (referring to both humanity and the ultimate man, Jesus). What evidences of this have you observed in the world and in your own life?

What truth from 2:9 is also expressed in 1 Timothy 2:6; 4:10; and Titus 2:11?

How does this truth equip you to talk about Jesus to people who are offended by what they perceive as the exclusivity of Christianity?

In what way was Jesus "made perfect" through suffering (2:10)?

Think about your own brother(s), if you have any, or about someone who has been a brother figure in your life. What is the significance of Jesus calling himself your brother (2:11)?

In what ways was Jesus qualified to be the author or pioneer (one who initiates and carries through) of salvation, as revealed in verses 9, 11, 14, and 18?

According to 2:11-18, in what ways does Jesus identify with human beings? How does this help you appreciate Jesus more?

In what way was the devil destroyed by Christ's death (2:14)?

In 2:17-18 we see that Jesus' humanity was essential for him to become our mediator (High Priest), the sacrifice for our sin, and our helper in overcoming sin. How can you appropriate and enjoy each of these three aspects of Christ's humanity?

According to 2:18, what are two specific experiences that Jesus has shared with us? What difference does it make in your life that he has shared these things with you?

CHAPTER 3

Take some time to read Hebrews 3:1–4:13 and work your way through the following questions before reading chapter 3.

How would you summarize what the transition ("therefore" or "and so") in 3:1 refers back to?

Based on the instruction in 3:1, in what practical ways can you "fix your thoughts on," "consider," or "think carefully about" Jesus?

In what ways is Jesus similar to and superior to Moses according to 3:1-6?

Similar	Superior

Why was Moses so esteemed by the Hebrew people? Why was it important for the Hebrews to see that Jesus is greater than Moses? (See John 1:17 for insight.)

Who or what do you tend to esteem too highly–someone or something that could threaten to take priority over the authority and influence of Jesus in your life?

What do you think it means to "hold fast our confidence" or "hold on to our courage and the hope of which we boast" (3:6)?

Describe what a person is like who fails to hold on to the courage and hope provided for us in Christ.

Read Hebrews 3:7-14, along with Exodus 17:1-7 and Numbers 20:1-13, which describe the two events referred to in Psalm 95, quoted in Hebrews 3. What did the people in the wilderness do wrong? What was the result for them?

What is the warning in this passage? Who is it for? What are the results of not heeding this warning?

In the series of questions found in 3:16-18, we discover that the people rebelled, sinned, and disobeyed. How are these attitudes and actions related to unbelief (3:19)?

While we don't like to label ourselves as "rebellious" against God, are there areas in which you would have to admit you have rebelled against him?

From reading through Hebrews 3 and 4, what was the "rest" God offered to the Israelites?

What rest is offered to us as believers to experience here and now?

What rest is still ahead for believers?

What is the implied warning of 4:2?

According to 4:2-3, how does a person enter God's rest?

How do you reconcile the offer of rest with the command in 4:11 to "make every effort" to enter that rest? How are both true in the life of a Christian?

In what ways would you like to have more rest in your spiritual life?

Read 4:12 in two or three different translations. What are at least four things you learn about God's Word from this verse?

CHAPTER 4

Take some time to read Hebrews 4:14–5:10; 7:1-28 and work your way through the following questions before reading chapter 4.

What are six things the writer tells you about Jesus in 4:14-16? Tell how each one is meaningful to you.

1.

2.

3.

4.

5.

6.

According to 4:14-16, what specific things are we to do because we have such a High Priest? What do these things mean to you in practical terms?

In what specific area of your life do you sense a special need to "approach the throne of grace"? Based on this passage, how do you anticipate being received?

Read Leviticus 16:1-34. What key words would you use to describe the ancient Jewish sacrificial system and the work of a priest?

What does Hebrews 5:1-4 teach about:

the work of a high priest?

the attitude of a high priest?

the appointment of a high priest to office?

From 5:7-10, what were the results of Christ's obedience?

What is an area in which you are tempted to disobey? What blessing for others might result from your obedience in this area?

Read Genesis 14:17-20 and Psalm 110:1-5 for the Old Testament background on Melchizedek. Then list some of the key facts given about Melchizedek in Hebrews 7:1-3.

In what ways was Jesus similar to Melchizedek according to 7:1-3, 15-17?

What was the author trying to convince the Hebrews of in his question in 7:11?

According to verse 16, what is the unique qualification of Jesus that was common to Melchizedek but not to the priestly descendents of Aaron?

In 7:18-19, what conclusion does the writer come to about the law? What conclusion does he come to about our "better hope"?

What did the Old Testament high priests do that Jesus never had to do (7:27)?

What did Jesus do that the Old Testament high priests never did (7:27)?

Note the descriptions and qualifications of Jesus in 7:26-28. Verse 26 says this kind of high priest "meets our need." What fundamental need do you have that Jesus is uniquely equipped to meet?

CHAPTER 5

Take some time to read Hebrews 5:11–6:20 and work your way through the following questions before reading chapter 5.

What is the writer's frustration with the Jewish Christians, expressed in 5:11-14?

What are marks of spiritual maturity, according to 5:12-14?

What would you say is the root cause of any spiritual immaturity that you may have, and what are you willing to do about it?

What spiritual experiences are described in 6:4-6? How would you explain what each means?

Do you think it is possible for a person to be "enlightened," to "taste" and "partake" of God and yet not put faith in him for salvation? Why or why not?

What do the following verses indicate about the impossibility for someone who has genuinely partaken in the spiritual experiences described in verses 4-6 to fall away from faith?

John 10:27-29

Philippians 1:6

1 Peter 1:3-5

The writer says in verse 9 that he is "confident of better things in your case–things that accompany salvation." What does that imply about the spiritual condition of those described in 6:4-6?

What are these believers encouraged to do and what are they warned against doing in 6:9-12?

According to 6:13-18, what twofold basis is there for confidence in the truth and in the sure fulfillment of God's promises? What does this tell you about God?

In what way does placing your faith in the promises of God serve as an anchor for your soul (6:19)?

When have you held on to the promises of God as an anchor for your soul in the midst of a storm in your life?

What specific promise of God do you need to cling to this week? Where is this promise found in the Bible?

CHAPTER 6

Take some time to read Hebrews 8:1–10:18 and work your way through the following questions before reading chapter 6.

What does Hebrews 8:1-5 reveal about why such specific instructions were given in the Old Testament about the building of the Tabernacle?

What is superior to what in 8:6, and why?

In what specific ways, according to Jeremiah's prophecy quoted in 8:8-12, does the new covenant differ from the old?

Which aspects of the way God relates to us under the new covenant (8:10-12) are most meaningful to you personally?

What were the duties of the priests in the Tabernacle, and where did they carry them out (9:6-7, 13)?

Considering that God dwelled in the Most Holy Place in the Hebrew Tabernacle, what are some practical ways our experience with God is different from that of the Hebrews under the old covenant?

According to 9:9-10, why couldn't the gifts and sacrifices offered in the Tabernacle clear the conscience of the worshipper?

What is it like to live with a guilty conscience? How have you experienced the freedom of a clear and cleansed conscience?

According to 9:11-14, what does the blood of Christ do that animals' blood could not do?

According to 9:15-22, for what two reasons did Christ have to die?

What is the warning/promise in 9:27-28?

According to 10:1-4, in what three ways did the sacrifices of the Old Testament prove inadequate?

What does the quotation from Psalm 40 in 10:5-10 reveal about King David's understanding of the sacrificial system?

From 10:11-18, what is the significance that Jesus died once for all?

CHAPTER 7

Take some time to read Hebrews 10:19-39 and work your way through the following questions before reading chapter 7.

Until now, the writer to the Hebrews has been telling us what God has done. Now he transitions into what we are to do in light of what God has done for us through Christ. Read 10:19-25. What four things does the writer exhort us to do?

What examples have you seen of believers who live this way?

In what specific way could you apply these four exhortations to your own life?

Read 10:26-31. What is the warning, and who is this warning for?

According to 10:29, what are those who deliberately continue to sin doing to the Son of God?

According to 10:32-34, what had these Christians experienced in earlier days? How did they respond, and what enabled them to respond that way?

According to 10:35-39, what choices are open to us when we are persecuted for our faith? What are the consequences of each choice?

In what ways have you experienced suffering, insult, persecution, or loss?

In what area of your life do you need to persevere right now?

When a friend is discouraged in her faith walk, how can you encourage her to persevere in obeying and trusting God, based on this passage?

CHAPTER 8

Take some time to read Hebrews 11 and work your way through the following questions before reading chapter 8.

What are some ways people today define faith?

Based on Hebrews 11:1, how would you define faith (in your own words)?

In what ways did God enable each of these people to live out their deep confidence in God's promises?

Abel

Enoch

Noah

Abraham

Isaac

Jacob

Joseph

Moses

Israelites

Rahab

List at least six characteristics that describe the people of faith mentioned in 11:13-16.

Do you find yourself longing for a better country–a heavenly one? If so, what are you most looking forward to? If not, why do you think that is?

According to 11:24-28, what specific things did Moses believe that influenced his actions?

In what way do the experiences of faith in verses 35b-38 stand as a stark contrast to the faith achievements described in 32-35a?

According to 11:39-40, what three things were true for both the victorious and the suffering heroes?

Finish this sentence: I want my life of faith to be marked by . . .

CHAPTER 9

Take some time to read Hebrews 12:1-24 and work your way through the following questions before reading chapter 9.

To whom does the "great cloud of witnesses" in 12:1 refer? And what are these witnesses testifying about?

Who are some people whose lives serve as a witness to you about how to run your faith race well? What is it about their example that encourages you?

According to 12:1-3, state as specifically as you can

what we must reject

how we should run

where we must focus

What are some of the weights that drag people down in their spiritual journeys?

Are there certain sins you find yourself falling into over and over again? (You may not want to share this in a group discussion, but identifying it for yourself and writing it down is the first step toward overcoming it.)

How can considering carefully the description of Jesus in 12:2-3 keep us from giving up when things are hard?

What perspective does 12:4 offer to us in our struggles against sin?

According to 12:5-11, how should we think about and respond to the difficulties in our lives?

According to 12:5-13, what are the benefits of responding in submission to God's discipline?

According to 12:12-17, what actions are Christians urged to take in order to persevere in the race of faith? Which one of these actions do you want to work on this week?

How does Deuteronomy 29:18 help us understand what the writer means by a "bitter root" that can "cause trouble and defile many" (12:15)? How is Esau an example of this (see 12:16-17)?

Read Exodus 19:12-13 and Deuteronomy 4:11-13, which describe the Israelites approaching God to receive the Law on Mount Sinai. In what way was that different from the new way believers are invited to approach God in 12:18-25?

CHAPTER 10

Take some time to read Hebrews 12:25–13:25 and work your way through the following questions before reading chapter 10.

What is the warning in verse 25? What actions can you take to heed this warning?

According to verse 28, how are we to respond to being given a "kingdom that cannot be shaken"? Can you think of a situation in your life when God gave you the faith to respond in one of these ways?

According to Hebrews 13:1-6, what are at least five qualities that should characterize us as Christians in our day-to-day lives?

1.
2.
3.
4.
5.

Which of these qualities would you like to develop more fully? What could you do to make them more of a reality in your life?

How does this list of practical matters of the Christian life relate to the main message of the letter to the Hebrews?

What is the message of 13:7 and 17? What is a specific way you can obey this instruction over the coming days and weeks?

What are ways we can honor our spiritual leaders even if we don't agree with them?

What are ways we make the work of our spiritual leaders a joy? How do we make it a burden?

What does it mean to "continually offer to God a sacrifice of praise," as described in 13:15-16? In what situations or circumstances do you find it especially difficult to obey this instruction?

Take a few moments to use the prayer in 13:20-21 for others in your group or in your family. What are you asking God to do for them? What are you asking God to do in them?

If someone asked you what the book of Hebrews is about, how would you summarize it?

What is the most potentially life-changing truth you have learned in this study of Hebrews?

How has this study changed a belief, an attitude, or a behavior in your life?

So, my dear Christian friends,
companions in following this call to the heights,
take a good hard look at Jesus.

He's the centerpiece of everything we believe.

HEBREWS 3:1 (*The Message*)

NOTES

1. John MacArthur, *The MacArthur New Testament Commentary: Hebrews* (Chicago: Moody Press, 1983), 14.
2. Tim Keller, "Christ: The Final Word" (sermon, Redeemer Presbyterian Church, New York, February 6, 2005).
3. MacArthur, 44.
4. Keller, "Christ: The Final Word."
5. John Piper, "Who Will Rule the World to Come?" (sermon, Bethlehem Baptist Church, Minneapolis, MN, May 19, 1996).
6. MacArthur, 70.
7. John Piper, "Jesus Is Able to Help Those Who Are Tempted" (sermon, Bethlehem Baptist Church, Minneapolis, MN, June 23, 1996).
8. Tim Keller, "The Rest Giver" (sermon, Redeemer Presbyterian Church, New York, February 20, 2005).
9. C. S. Lewis, *Mere Christianity* (New York: Macmillan, 1952), 124–125.
10. John Piper, "He Is the Source of Eternal Salvation for All Who Obey Him" (sermon, Bethlehem Baptist Church, Minneapolis, MN, September 22, 1996).
11. MacArthur, 177.
12. John Piper, "Jesus: From Melchizedek to Eternal Savior" (sermon, Bethlehem Baptist Church, Minneapolis, MN, December 1, 1996).
13. Ibid.
14. Arthur W. Pink, *An Exposition of Hebrews* (Grand Rapids, MI: Baker Books, 2003), chapter 23.
15. R. Kent Hughes, *Hebrews: An Anchor for the Soul* (Wheaton, IL: Crossway Books), 1:154.
16. John Piper, "Let Us Press On to Maturity" (sermon, Bethlehem Baptist Church, Minneapolis, MN, October 6, 1996).
17. MacArthur, 146–147.
18. Samuel Macauley Jackson, ed., *Schaff-Herzog Encyclopedia of Religious Knowledge* (New York: Funk & Wagnalls, 1914), 1:562.
19. MacArthur, 239.
20. Hughes, 1:233–234.
21. According to Hughes, 234, "During the Passover, for example, a trough was constructed

from the Temple down into the Kidron Valley for the disposal of blood—a sacrificial plumbing system."

22. Hughes, 1:228.

23. John Piper, "Purified to Serve the Living God" (sermon, Bethlehem Baptist Church, Minneapolis, MN, January 12, 1997).

24. MacArthur, 249.

25. John Piper, "What Christ Did at the End of the Age" (sermon, Bethlehem Baptist Church, Minneapolis, MN, February 7, 1997).

26. From an unnamed article quoted by Dean Angell in "Guilty Conscience" (sermon, Lakeview Church, Saskatoon, SK, Canada, March 16, 2002).

27. The Voice of the Martyrs News, "Nearly 50 Chinese House Church Leaders Arrested at Retreat and Released," October 21, 2005.

Books by Nancy Guthrie

Holding On to Hope
978-1-4143-1296-5

Hearing Jesus Speak
into Your Sorrow
978-1-4143-2548-4

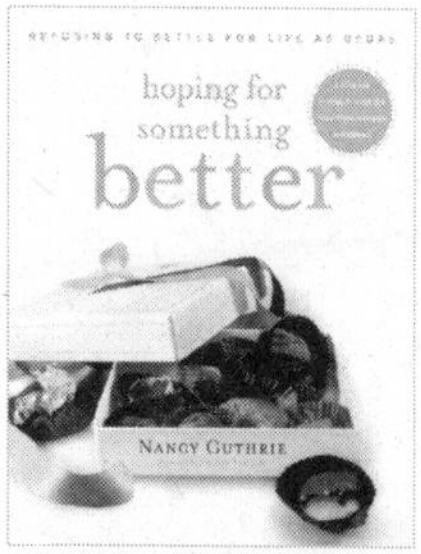

Hoping for Something Better
978-1-4143-1307-8

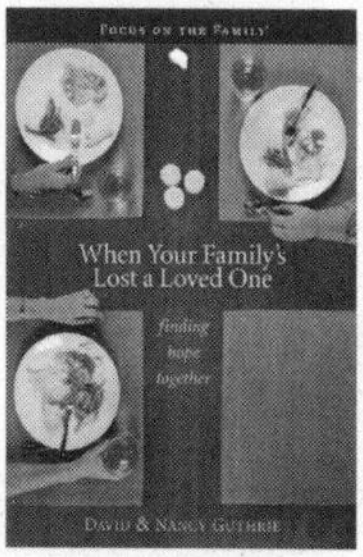

When Your Family's
Lost a Loved One
978-1-58997-480-7

The One Year Book of Hope
978-1-4143-0133-4(softcover)
978-1-4143-3671-8(leatherlike)

One Year of Dinner Table
Devotions and Discussion
Starters
978-1-4143-1895-0

Let Every Heart Prepare
Him Room
978-1-4143-3909-2

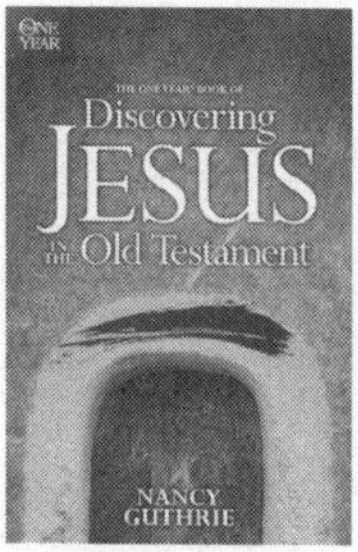

The One Year Book of
Discovering Jesus in the
Old Testament
978-1-4143-3590-2

Abundant Life in Jesus
978-1-4964-0948-5

For more information on these titles, visit www.tyndale.com or www.nancyguthrie.com.
For information about David and Nancy Guthrie's Respite Retreats for couples who have faced the loss of a child, go to www.nancyguthrie.com/respite-retreat.

CP0066